donna hay

THE NEW
easy

135+ clever solutions and flavour-packed recipes for weeknights and weekends

HarperCollins*Publishers*

CONTENTS

BAKING
page 138

DESSERTS
page 164

GLOSSARY AND INDEX
page 190

*Ingredients marked with an asterisk have a glossary entry

INTRODUCTION

This book is all about new ways to make cooking easier. It features new flavour combinations and new shortcuts, designed to simplify life in the kitchen. It captures how most of us, including me, like to cook – with quick solutions for busy weeknights, and special dishes for weekends when you have more time up your sleeve. Each chapter contains clever and versatile ideas to put a spin on some of your favourites. So once you've mastered a dish, I've included a new section called 're-style', showing you how to transform it into a chic starter for a dinner party, say, or a handy addition to a picnic. Happy cooking!

WEEKNIGHTS

This collection of recipes is my solution to the midweek dilemma of what to cook that's simple and satisfying. It's big on new flavours and shortcuts, making busy weeknights so much easier.

crispy spiced kale <small>AND</small> chicken salad

tomato tarts WITH burrata AND prosciutto

crispy spiced kale AND chicken salad

10 stalks kale, stems removed
2 generous tablespoons extra virgin olive oil
2 teaspoons sea salt flakes
1 teaspoon smoked paprika*
1 teaspoon ground coriander
320g shredded cooked chicken
45g slivered almonds, toasted
55g currants
5g flat-leaf parsley leaves
5g mint leaves
dressing
1 teaspoon smoked paprika*
1 generous tablespoon honey
1 generous tablespoon extra virgin olive oil
1 generous tablespoon lemon juice

Preheat oven to 180°C (350°F). To make the dressing, mix to combine the paprika, honey, oil and lemon juice and set aside.

Chop the kale into large pieces and place on baking trays lined with non-stick baking paper. Add the oil and toss to coat. Combine the salt, paprika and coriander and sprinkle over the kale. Bake for 10–15 minutes or until the kale is crisp. Cool on trays.

Divide the kale, chicken, almonds, currants, parsley and mint leaves between plates and spoon over the dressing to serve. SERVES 4

tomato tarts WITH burrata AND prosciutto

4 sheets (680g) store-bought puff pastry, thawed
500g mixed heirloom or vine cherry tomatoes
1 tablespoon extra virgin olive oil
3 cloves garlic, sliced
2 tablespoons oregano leaves
sea salt and cracked black pepper
1 burrata*, halved
8 slices prosciutto
2 tablespoons small mint leaves
2 tablespoons small basil leaves

Preheat oven to 200°C (400°F). Cut 4 x 20cm rounds from the pastry. Place 2 rounds on baking trays lined with non-stick baking paper, top with the remaining 2 rounds and press to secure.

Cut a slit in the side of each tomato and squeeze to release the juice and seeds. Place the tomatoes, oil, garlic, oregano, salt and pepper in a bowl and toss to combine. Divide the tomatoes between the pastry bases and bake for 15–20 minutes or until the pastry is golden. Top the tarts with the burrata, prosciutto, mint and basil to serve. SERVES 4

chicken bolognese WITH crispy oregano

2 generous tablespoons extra virgin olive oil
25g oregano leaves
1 onion, finely chopped
3 cloves garlic, crushed
1 heaped tablespoon chopped tarragon
500g chicken mince
250ml dry white wine
2 x 400g tins chopped tomatoes
sea salt and cracked black pepper
400g pappardelle
finely grated Pecorino, to serve

Heat the oil in a large non-stick frying pan over medium heat. Add the oregano and cook for 1–2 minutes or until crispy. Remove with a slotted spoon and set aside. Add the onion, garlic and tarragon to the pan and cook, stirring, for 3–4 minutes or until softened. Add the chicken mince and cook, breaking up any lumps with a wooden spoon, for 5–7 minutes or until golden. Add the wine, tomatoes, salt and pepper and cook for 5–7 minutes or until reduced.

Cook the pasta in a large saucepan of boiling salted water for 8–10 minutes or until al dente. Drain, add to the sauce and toss to combine. Divide the pasta between bowls and top with the crispy oregano and pecorino to serve. SERVES 4

chicken bolognese WITH crispy oregano

greek lemon yoghurt skewers

tarragon AND lemon roasted chicken

greek lemon yoghurt skewers

280g plain Greek-style yoghurt
1 generous tablespoon extra virgin olive oil
1 heaped tablespoon finely grated lemon zest
2 heaped tablespoons chopped oregano leaves
2 heaped tablespoons chopped mint leaves
2 heaped tablespoons chopped dill leaves
2 teaspoons ground cumin
sea salt and cracked black pepper
8 x 125g chicken thigh fillets, halved
sliced celery, mint leaves, lemon wedges and labne*, to serve
1 teaspoon dried mint

Place the yoghurt, oil, lemon zest, oregano, mint, dill, cumin, salt and pepper in a large bowl and mix to combine. Add the chicken and toss to coat. Refrigerate for 1 hour to marinate.

Thread the chicken onto double skewers and cook under a preheated hot grill for 10–12 minutes or until browned and cooked through. Divide the skewers between plates, sprinkle with the dried mint and serve with the celery, mint, lemon and labne. SERVES 4

A simple marinade of tangy yoghurt, zesty lemon, fresh dill and mint is all it takes to give these skewers plenty of flavour.

tarragon AND lemon roasted chicken

1.8kg chicken pieces on the bone
1 generous tablespoon extra virgin olive oil
sea salt and cracked black pepper
10 small sprigs tarragon
1 heaped tablespoon shredded lemon zest
3 cloves garlic, sliced
2 fennel bulbs, trimmed and sliced
125ml dry white wine
125ml chicken stock
lemon wedges, to serve

Preheat oven to 180°C (350°F). Heat a heavy-based ovenproof casserole dish on the hob over high heat. Score the chicken skin at regular intervals, drizzle with the oil, sprinkle with salt and pepper and toss to coat. Add to the dish and cook for 6–8 minutes each side or until well browned. Remove from the pan and set aside. Add the tarragon, lemon, garlic and fennel to the dish and cook for 2–3 minutes or until golden. Return the chicken to the dish with the wine and stock and bring to a simmer. Transfer to the oven and roast for 20–25 minutes or until the chicken is just cooked through. Serve with the lemon wedges. SERVES 4

crispy cauliflower pasta

700g cauliflower, trimmed and roughly chopped
80g pine nuts
60ml extra virgin olive oil
2 cloves garlic, chopped
7g oregano leaves
2 heaped tablespoons finely grated lemon zest
1 teaspoon dried chilli flakes
sea salt and cracked black pepper
400g orecchiette
grated Parmesan or Pecorino, to serve

Place the cauliflower and pine nuts in a food processor and process until finely chopped. Heat a large non-stick frying pan over medium-high heat. Add the oil, garlic, cauliflower mixture, oregano, lemon zest, chilli, salt and pepper and cook, stirring occasionally, for 15 minutes or until the cauliflower is golden. While the cauliflower is cooking, cook the pasta in a large saucepan of salted boiling water for 8–10 minutes or until al dente. Drain.

Toss the pasta with the cauliflower mixture and sprinkle with the cheese to serve. SERVES 4

crispy cauliflower pasta

lemongrass chicken salad

lemongrass chicken salad

1 stalk lemongrass*, trimmed and finely chopped
6 kaffir lime leaves*, finely sliced
1 heaped tablespoon finely grated ginger
2 teaspoons caster sugar
1 generous tablespoon fish sauce*
1 generous tablespoon vegetable oil
2 x 160g chicken breast fillets, each cut into 3 pieces
1 baby cos (romaine) lettuce, leaves separated
2 long green chillies, seeds removed and shredded
½ cucumber, peeled and chopped
45g roasted salted peanuts
baby coriander leaves, to serve
lime dressing
3 generous tablespoons lime juice
1 generous tablespoon fish sauce*
2 teaspoons brown sugar

To make the lime dressing, mix to combine the lime juice, fish sauce and sugar and set aside.

Place the lemongrass, lime leaves, ginger, sugar, fish sauce and oil in a bowl and mix to combine. Add the chicken and toss to coat. Allow to stand for 5–15 minutes to marinate.

Preheat a char-grill pan or barbecue over medium-high heat. Cook the chicken for 2–3 minutes each side or until cooked through. Divide the chicken and cos leaves between plates and top with the chilli, cucumber and peanuts. Drizzle with the dressing and sprinkle with the coriander to serve. SERVES 4

RE-STYLE

WEEKEND PICNIC *portable lunch*
To make sandwiches, spread crispy baguettes with mayonnaise and top with the lemongrass chicken, lettuce, cucumber and chilli to serve.

ELEGANT STARTER *for a party*
Slice the cooked chicken into thin pieces and place in cos lettuce cups with the chilli, cucumber and peanuts. Spoon over the dressing just before serving.

pork AND fennel sausage pasta

white pepper grilled chicken

goat's cheese frittata WITH rocket gremolata

pork AND fennel sausage pasta

400g casarecce or penne
1 generous tablespoon extra virgin olive oil
4 (400g) pork and fennel sausages, skins removed
1 small red chilli, chopped
1 teaspoon finely grated lemon zest
2 baby fennel bulbs, trimmed and finely sliced
60ml dry white wine
125ml chicken stock
2 heaped tablespoons flat-leaf parsley leaves
grated Parmesan or Pecorino, to serve

Cook the pasta in a large saucepan of salted boiling water for 8–10 minutes or until al dente. While the pasta is cooking, heat the oil a large non-stick frying pan over medium-high heat. Break off small pieces of the sausages and cook for 4–5 minutes each side or until cooked through. Add the chilli, lemon, fennel, wine and stock and simmer for 5 minutes. Add the cooked and drained pasta and toss to combine. Divide between serving bowls and sprinkle with the parsley and cheese to serve. SERVES 4

white pepper grilled chicken

1 heaped tablespoon white peppercorns
2 teaspoons sea salt flakes
1 teaspoon fennel seeds
4 x 200g chicken breast fillets, bone in, skin on
1 generous tablespoon extra virgin olive oil
parsley salad
1 generous tablespoon red wine vinegar
2 teaspoons honey
1 generous tablespoon vegetable oil
60g flat-leaf parsley leaves, roughly chopped
2 heaped tablespoons salted capers, rinsed
⅓ cucumber, peeled and thinly sliced

Preheat oven to 180°C (350°F). To make the parsley salad, mix to combine the vinegar, honey and oil. Place the parsley, capers and cucumber in a bowl and toss to combine. Set both aside.

Preheat a barbecue or char-grill pan over medium-low heat. Place the peppercorns, salt and fennel seeds into a mortar and grind with a pestle until the mixture is a rough powder. Score the chicken skin at regular intervals, brush with oil and sprinkle with the white pepper mixture. Cook the chicken for 5 minutes each side or until golden.

Transfer to a baking tray, skin-side up, and roast for 15–20 minutes or until the chicken is cooked through. Serve with the parsley salad and dressing. SERVES 4

goat's cheese frittata WITH rocket gremolata

8 eggs
250ml single cream*
250ml milk
80g finely grated Parmesan
sea salt and cracked black pepper
200g soft goat's cheese or goat's curd*
2 teaspoons lemon thyme leaves
rocket gremolata
90g rocket leaves, shredded
20g flat-leaf parsley leaves, finely chopped
1 heaped tablespoon finely grated lemon zest
1 generous tablespoon extra virgin olive oil

Preheat oven to 180°C (350°F). To make the rocket gremolata, place the rocket, parsley, lemon zest and oil in a bowl and stir to combine. Set aside.

Place the eggs, cream, milk, parmesan, salt and pepper in a bowl and whisk to combine. Pour into a 1.5-litre-capacity ovenproof dish. Top the frittata with spoonfuls of goat's cheese and sprinkle with the thyme.

Bake for 25–30 minutes or until the frittata is almost set. Remove from the oven and stand for 5 minutes. Cut the frittata into wedges and serve with the gremolata. SERVES 4

A simple combination of egg and goat's cheese creates this smooth, velvety frittata. Zesty gremolata gives it a fresh kick.

dukkah-crusted schnitzels

baked pancetta AND parmesan chicken

dukkah-crusted schnitzels

135g store-bought dukkah*
70g fresh breadcrumbs
150g plain flour
3 eggs, lightly beaten
4 x 160g chicken breast fillets, halved horizontally
vegetable oil, for shallow frying
lemon wedges and store-bought aïoli*, to serve
radish salad
8 red radishes, thinly sliced
1 baby fennel bulb, thinly sliced
10g small flat-leaf parsley leaves
2 generous tablespoons extra virgin olive oil
1 generous tablespoon lemon juice
sea salt and cracked black pepper

Combine the dukkah and breadcrumbs and place in a shallow
bowl. Place the flour and the egg in separate shallow bowls.
Coat the chicken in the flour, shaking to remove any excess,
dip in the egg mixture and press into the crumb mixture.
   Heat the oil in a large non-stick frying pan over medium heat.
Cook the schnitzels for 3–4 minutes each side or until golden
and cooked through. Drain on absorbent paper.
   To make the radish salad, combine the radish, fennel and
parsley in a bowl. Whisk together the oil, lemon juice, salt and
pepper, pour over the salad and toss to combine. Serve the
schnitzels with the salad, lemon wedges and aïoli. SERVES 4

baked pancetta AND parmesan chicken

8 slices pancetta*
8 sprigs oregano
4 x 160g chicken breast fillets, trimmed
160g finely grated Parmesan
70g fresh breadcrumbs
sea salt and cracked black pepper
2 generous tablespoons extra virgin olive oil
rocket leaves, halved cherry tomatoes and basil leaves,
   to serve

Preheat oven to 220°C (425°F). Place 4 slices of pancetta
on a baking tray. Top each slice with an oregano sprig and a
chicken breast. Combine the Parmesan, breadcrumbs, salt and
pepper and sprinkle generously over the chicken. Top with the
remaining oregano and pancetta. Drizzle with the oil and bake
for 10–14 minutes or until the chicken is cooked through and
the pancetta is golden and crisp. Serve with the rocket, tomatoes
and basil. SERVES 4

brussels sprout AND brown butter pasta

400g spaghetti
85g butter
1 generous tablespoon extra virgin olive oil
10g small sage leaves
70g chopped hazelnuts
700g Brussels sprouts, trimmed and quartered
2 cloves garlic, crushed
sea salt and cracked black pepper
lemon wedges, to serve

Cook the pasta in a large saucepan of salted boiling water
for 8–10 minutes or until al dente. Drain and set aside.
   While the pasta is cooking, heat the butter and oil in a large
non-stick frying pan over medium-high heat. Add the sage and
hazelnuts and cook for 2–3 minutes or until golden. Add the sprouts,
garlic, salt and pepper and cook, turning, for 3–4 minutes or until
just soft and golden.
   Divide the pasta between bowls, top with the sprout mixture
and serve with the lemon wedges. SERVES 4

brussels sprout AND brown butter pasta

pepper steaks

pepper steaks

2 heaped tablespoons green peppercorns in brine*, drained
4 shallots, peeled and chopped
1 heaped tablespoon tarragon leaves
4 x 150g sirloin steaks, trimmed
sea salt
1 generous tablespoon extra virgin olive oil
60g butter

Place the peppercorns, shallots and tarragon in a small food processor and process until finely chopped. Set aside.

Sprinkle the steaks with salt. Heat a large non-stick frying pan over high heat. Add the oil, butter and peppercorn mixture and cook for 1 minute. Add the steaks and cook for 2–3 minutes each side or until well browned and cooked to your liking.

Divide between plates and spoon over the pan sauce. Serve with thick-cut potato chips, if desired. SERVES 4

RE-STYLE

MAKE IT CHIC *dinner party*

For an elegant presentation, place the steak on top of rocket leaves. Stack the chips in a neat grid and serve with aïoli* in individual bowls.

TASTY LUNCH *in a sandwich*

Halve a long Turkish bread loaf or ciabatta, spread the base with aïoli* and top with the pepper steak. Top with caramelised onion relish* and sandwich with the top of the loaf. Cut into pieces to serve.

chicken waldorf

grilled cavolo nero AND ricotta salad

veal AND sage meatloaves

chicken waldorf

140g plain yoghurt
2 generous tablespoons white balsamic vinegar
sea salt and cracked black pepper
2 fennel bulbs, thinly sliced
2 Granny Smith apples, thinly sliced
480g shredded cooked chicken
10g mint leaves
candied walnuts
55g white sugar
60ml red wine vinegar
¼ teaspoon sea salt flakes
100g walnuts

To make the candied walnuts, place the sugar and vinegar in a large non-stick frying pan over medium-high heat and stir until the sugar dissolves. Simmer for 3–4 minutes, stirring ocassionally, or until the sugar has caramelised and is light golden. Add the sea salt flakes with the walnuts and toss to coat. Transfer to a baking tray lined with non-stick baking paper and allow to cool.

Mix to combine the yoghurt, balsamic, salt and pepper and set aside. Place the fennel, apple, chicken and mint in a bowl and toss to combine. Divide the salad between plates, sprinkle with the walnuts and serve with the dressing. SERVES 4

grilled cavolo nero AND ricotta salad

16 stalks cavolo nero, trimmed
2 generous tablespoons extra virgin olive oil
3 medium (360g) courgettes, shredded
25g shredded mint leaves
100g ricotta salata*, finely sliced
lemon honey dressing
60ml lemon juice
2 generous tablespoons extra virgin olive oil
1 generous tablespoon honey
1 heaped tablespoon Dijon mustard

Preheat a barbecue or char-grill pan over medium-high heat. To make the lemon honey dressing, whisk together the lemon juice, oil, honey, mustard, salt and pepper and set aside.

Cut the cavolo nero in half, place in a bowl with the oil and toss to coat. Cook for 30 seconds–1 minute each side or until slightly charred and crisp. Set aside. Divide the courgette, mint and ricotta between plates, drizzle with the dressing and top with the cavolo nero to serve. SERVES 4

veal AND sage meatloaves

800g veal mince
1 clove garlic, crushed
2 heaped tablespoons chopped sage
1 heaped tablespoon quince paste*
135g grated Granny Smith apple
1 heaped tablespoon Dijon mustard
2 eggs
70g fresh breadcrumbs
1 teaspoon ground allspice
sea salt and cracked black pepper
12 slices pancetta*
mustard and fried sage leaves, to serve
quince glaze
2 heaped tablespoons quince paste*
2 generous tablespoons boiling water
1 generous tablespoon maple syrup

Preheat oven to 180°C (350°F). Place the mince, garlic, sage, quince paste, apple, mustard, eggs, breadcrumbs, allspice, salt and pepper in a bowl and mix until well combined. Line a 12 x 125ml cups lightly greased muffin tin with the pancetta. Spoon in the mince mixture and bake for 15 minutes or until just cooked. Turn out onto a baking tray lined with non-stick baking paper.

To make the quince glaze, combine the quince paste, water and maple syrup. Brush over the meatloaves, return to the oven and bake for a further 5 minutes or until golden. Serve with mustard and fried sage leaves. SERVES 4-6

courgette AND feta pancakes

goat's cheese, pear AND pancetta tarts

courgette AND feta pancakes

810g courgettes, grated
3 eggs
250g feta, roughly chopped
120g plain flour
1½ teaspoons baking powder
7g chopped mint leaves
10g chopped flat-leaf parsley leaves
sea salt and cracked black pepper
extra virgin olive oil, for frying
tomato salad
2 teaspoons honey
2 generous tablespoons lemon juice
350g mixed cherry tomatoes, halved
20g small basil leaves
2 heaped tablespoons small mint leaves

Place the courgette in a flat layer on sheets of absorbent paper.
Cover with another layer of paper and press to remove the excess
water. Place the courgette, eggs, feta, flour, baking powder, mint,
parsley, salt and pepper in a bowl and mix to combine.

Heat a little of the oil in a large non-stick frying pan over
medium-high heat. Add 2 tablespoons of mixture to the
pan and flatten with a spatula. Repeat and cook, in batches,
for 2–3 minutes each side or until golden. Keep the pancakes
warm and set aside.

To make the tomato salad, place the honey, lemon juice, salt
and pepper in a bowl and stir to combine. Add the tomato, basil
and mint and toss to combine. Divide the pancakes between
plates and top with the tomato salad to serve. **SERVES 4**

goat's cheese, pear AND pancetta tarts

2 sheets (400g) store-bought shortcrust pasty*, thawed
200g firm goat's cheese*, sliced
1 firm pear, cut into thin wedges
16 thin slices pancetta*
16 thyme sprigs
30g butter, melted
2 generous tablespoons maple syrup
cracked black pepper

Preheat oven to 200°C (400°F). Trim the edges of the pastry
and cut into four 24cm x 12cm rectangles. Place on a baking
tray lined with non-stick baking paper. Top the tarts with goat's
cheese, pear, pancetta and thyme sprigs. Combine the butter
and maple syrup and drizzle over the tarts. Sprinkle with pepper
and bake for 15–20 minutes or until the pastry is golden. **SERVES 4**

carrot AND red lentil soup

2 generous tablespoons extra virgin olive oil
1 onion, finely chopped
2 cloves garlic, crushed
2 teaspoons finely grated ginger
1 heaped tablespoon harissa paste*
2 teaspoons ground coriander
4 carrots, peeled and grated
200g red lentils
1.5 litres chicken stock
plain yoghurt and mint leaves, to serve
harissa toasts
8 thin slices sourdough bread
2 teaspoons harissa paste*
extra virgin olive oil, for drizzling

Heat a large saucepan over medium-high heat. Add the oil,
onion, garlic and ginger and cook, stirring, for 4 minutes or
until the onion is soft. Add the harissa and coriander and cook
for 1 minute. Add the carrot, lentils and stock, and bring to the
boil. Cover and simmer for 12 minutes, stirring occasionally,
so the lentils do not stick to the base of the pan.

While the soup is cooking, make the harissa toasts. Spread the
bread with a little harissa, drizzle with oil and grill under a preheated
hot grill until golden and crisp.

Divide the soup between bowls and serve with the harissa
toasts, yoghurt and mint. **SERVES 4**

carrot AND red lentil soup

crispy salmon <u>with</u> dill pickled onions

crispy salmon WITH dill pickled onions

1 teaspoon dried chilli flakes
1 teaspoon sea salt flakes
2 teaspoons sesame seeds
1 teaspoon dried mint
4 x 180g pieces salmon fillet, skin on
extra virgin olive oil, for brushing
baby spinach leaves and extra dill sprigs, to serve
dill pickled onions
2 red onions, finely sliced
80ml lemon juice
2 heaped tablespoons caster sugar
5g dill sprigs
sea salt and cracked black pepper

To make the dill pickled onions, place the onion, lemon juice, sugar, dill and a generous amount of salt and pepper in a bowl and toss well to combine. Set aside.

Combine the chilli, salt, sesame and mint. Brush the salmon lightly with oil and sprinkle the flesh-side only with the spice mixture. Heat a large non-stick frying pan over high heat. Add the salmon, skin-side down, and cook for 5 minutes or until the skin is crispy. Turn the salmon and cook for a further 2–3 minutes or until cooked to your liking.

Divide the salmon between plates and top with the dill pickled onions. Toss the baby spinach leaves with a little of the pickling liquid and serve with the fish. SERVES 4

RE-STYLE

CHIC PICNIC *take it away*

Cut the salmon into large chunks and toss with cooked and cooled rice noodles, baby spinach leaves, extra dill, the pickled onions and their dressing.

DINNER PARTY *smart starter*

Cut the salmon into large chunks and serve with a salad of baby spinach leaves, very thinly sliced fennel, micro herbs, the pickled onions and their dressing, and extra dill.

thai chicken salad <u>with</u> coconut dressing

simple beef noodle soup

thai chicken salad WITH coconut dressing

6 slices ginger
4 kaffir lime leaves*
4 slices lime
1.5 litres water
3 x 160g chicken breast fillets, trimmed
1 cucumber, peeled and chopped
500g cooked jasmine rice (200g uncooked)
20g mint leaves
30g coriander leaves
2 handfuls pea shoots
coconut dressing
200ml coconut cream*
25g coriander leaves, chopped
1 generous tablespoon fish sauce*
2 generous tablespoons lime juice
3 large green chillies, seeds removed and chopped
1 teaspoon caster sugar
2 kaffir lime leaves*

Place the ginger, lime leaves, lime and water in a deep frying pan over medium-high heat and simmer for 4 minutes. Add the chicken, reduce the heat to low and simmer for 8 minutes. Remove from the heat and stand for 5 minutes. Remove the chicken from the pan, shred and set aside.

To make the coconut dressing, place the coconut cream, coriander, fish sauce, lime juice, chilli, sugar and lime leaves in a small food processor and process until smooth.

Place the chicken, cucumber, rice, mint, coriander and snow pea shoots in a bowl and toss to combine. Divide between plates and serve with the dressing. SERVES 4

simple beef noodle soup

1.25 litres beef stock
1 heaped tablespoon shredded ginger
3 cloves garlic, sliced
1 star anise
1 cinnamon stick
180g egg noodles
1 x 300g piece fillet steak, thinly sliced
200g oyster mushrooms
1 white onion, peeled and very thinly sliced
15g Thai or ordinary basil leaves
5g Vietnamese mint or coriander leaves
180g bean sprouts, trimmed
2 large red or green chillies, sliced
lemon wedges, to serve

Place the stock, ginger, garlic, star anise and cinnamon in a saucepan and bring to the boil. Cover and simmer for 5 minutes.

Cook the noodles in a separate saucepan of boiling water for 2–3 minutes or until tender. Drain and divide the noodles between bowls.

Cook the beef in the broth, in batches, for 25–30 seconds until just cooked and pink. Top the noodles with the beef. Remove the star anise and cinnamon from the broth and discard. Add the mushrooms and cook for 1 minute. Divide the broth and mushrooms between the bowls and top with the onion, basil, mint and bean sprouts. Serve with chilli and lemon wedges. SERVES 4

lemon fish WITH crispy dill

50g butter
1 tablespoon extra virgin olive oil
3 cloves garlic, thickly sliced
2 large green chillies, seeds removed and chopped
2 tablespoons shredded lemon zest
4 x 175g firm white fish fillets, halved
sea salt and cracked black pepper
3 tablespoons extra virgin olive oil, extra
20g dill sprigs

Heat a large non-stick frying pan over medium-low heat. Add the butter, oil, garlic, chilli and lemon and cook, stirring occasionally, for 2–3 minutes or until soft. Increase the heat to medium, sprinkle the fish with salt and pepper and cook for 2–3 minutes each side or until cooked to your liking.

Heat the extra oil in a non-stick frying pan over medium-high heat. Cook the dill, in small batches, for 1–2 minutes or until crisp. Drain on absorbent paper. Top the fish with the crispy dill and serve with lemon wedges. SERVES 4

lemon fish <u>with</u> crispy dill

thai red curry mussels <u>with</u> coconut lime sambal

baked red curry chicken

baked red curry chicken

8 x 125g chicken thigh fillets, skin on
100g store-bought Thai red curry paste*
1 x 400ml tin coconut milk*
250ml chicken stock
1 generous tablespoon fish sauce*
4 kaffir lime leaves*
coriander and basil leaves, pea shoots and lime wedges, to serve
steamed greens and jasmine rice, to serve

Preheat oven to 220°C (425°F). Place the chicken, skin-side up, in a heavy-based ovenproof casserole dish. Combine the curry paste, coconut milk, stock and fish sauce and pour over the chicken. Add the lime leaves, cover with a lid and bake for 20 minutes. Remove the lid and bake for a further 20–25 minutes or until the chicken is cooked through and golden. Sprinkle with the coriander, basil, pea shoots and serve with lime wedges, steamed greens and jasmine rice. SERVES 4

thai red curry mussels
WITH coconut lime sambal

2 generous tablespoons groundnut oil
2 heaped tablespoons store-bought Thai red curry paste*
350ml coconut milk*
1 generous tablespoon fish sauce*
1kg mussels, scrubbed and cleaned
lime wedges and coriander leaves, to serve
coconut lime sambal
40g desiccated coconut*
1 generous tablespoon coconut milk*
1 teaspoon fish sauce*
10g coriander leaves, finely chopped
2 green chillies, seeds removed and finely chopped
1 heaped tablespoon finely grated lime zest
sea salt

To make the coconut lime sambal, place the coconut, coconut milk, fish sauce, coriander, chilli, lime zest and salt in a bowl and stir to combine. Set aside.

Heat the oil in a large saucepan over medium-high heat, add the curry paste and cook for 1–2 minutes or until fragrant. Add the coconut milk and fish sauce and bring to the boil. Add the mussels and cook, covered, for 2–3 minutes or until the mussels open. Divide the mussels and broth between bowls, sprinkle with the sambal and coriander and serve with the lime wedges. SERVES 4

chicken burgers

3 x 160g chicken breast fillets, each cut into 6 pieces
½ teaspoon dried chilli flakes
1 teaspoon finely grated lime zest
1 generous tablespoon lime juice
2 generous tablespoons extra virgin olive oil
8 slices light rye bread, toasted
rocket leaves and avocado wedges, to serve
coriander and tahini dressing
280g plain yoghurt
70g tahini paste*
60g coriander leaves
3 generous tablespoons lime juice
sea salt and cracked black pepper

To make the coriander and tahini dressing, place the yoghurt, tahini, coriander, lime juice, salt and pepper in a small food processor and process until smooth. Set aside.

Place the chicken, chilli, lime zest and juice in a bowl and toss to combine. Heat the oil in a large non-stick frying pan over high heat and cook the chicken for 2–3 minutes each side or until golden and cooked through.

To assemble the burgers, top half the bread slices with rocket leaves, chicken and avocado and spoon over the tahini dressing. Sandwich with the remaining bread slices to serve. SERVES 4

chicken burgers

spiced lamb AND tahini tart

spiced lamb AND tahini tart

4 large Lebanese flatbreads
520g store-bought hummus
600g lamb mince
1 heaped tablespoon dried mint
2 generous tablespoons honey
1 heaped tablespoon ras el hanout*
80g pine nuts
sea salt and cracked black pepper
yoghurt, sumac*, lemon wedges and mint leaves, to serve

Preheat oven to 200°C (400°F). Place the flatbreads on baking trays lined with non-stick baking paper. Spread the breads with hummus leaving a 2cm border. Combine the lamb, mint, honey, ras el hanout, pine nuts, salt and pepper and sprinkle over the hummus. Bake for 12–15 minutes or until the lamb is golden and cooked through. Top with yoghurt and sprinkle with the sumac and mint leaves. Serve with the lemon wedges. SERVES 4

RE-STYLE

FOLD OVER *handheld snack*
Fold over the tarts before baking for 14–16 minutes. Serve with the toppings on the side.

BITE-SIZED *finger food*
Make the tarts on rectangular thin flatbreads. Cut into small squares and bake for 10 minutes or until golden. Serve with a little of the topping on each square.

roasted squash AND chorizo salad

ham **AND** cheese piadinas

ham AND cheese piadinas

2 large Lebanese flatbreads
180g stracchino or mozzarella cheese*, sliced
8 slices prosciutto
extra virgin olive oil, for brushing
15g small basil leaves

Preheat oven to 200°C (400°F). Spread one half of each flatbread with the cheese and top with the prosciutto. Fold over the bread to enclose the filling, brush with oil and place on baking trays lined with non-stick baking paper. Top the flatbreads with a sheet of non-stick baking paper and weigh down with another baking tray to flatten. Bake for 15–20 minutes or until golden and crisp. Serve with the basil leaves. SERVES 4

crispy sesame-crusted tofu

800g firm tofu*, thickly sliced
100g panko (Japanese) breadcrumbs*
75g sesame seeds
sea salt and cracked black pepper
2 egg whites
vegetable oil, for shallow frying
steamed Tenderstem broccoli and kecap manis (sweet soy
    sauce), to serve
roasted chilli salt
2 teaspoons dried chilli flakes
½ teaspoon Sichuan peppercorns*
2 teaspoons sea salt flakes

To make the roasted chilli salt, place the chilli and Sichuan pepper in a small frying pan over medium heat. Cook for 1–2 minutes or until fragrant, transfer to a small food processor or a mortar and grind until well combined. Set aside.
    Cut the tofu into 8 and dry well on absorbent paper. Combine the breadcrumbs, sesame and a generous amount of salt and pepper in a shallow bowl. Place the egg white in a separate shallow bowl. Dip the tofu into the egg white and roll in the crumb mixture to coat. Heat 2–3cm of the oil in a large deep frying pan until it reaches 180°C (355°F) on a kitchen thermometer. Cook the tofu, in batches, for 2–3 minutes each side or until golden and crisp. Drain on absorbent paper.
    Divide the broccolini between plates, drizzle with the soy and top with the tofu. Sprinkle with the chilli salt to serve. SERVES 4

roasted squash AND chorizo salad

750g butternut squash, peeled and cut into chunks
6 shallots, peeled and quartered
1 generous tablespoon extra virgin olive oil
2 dried chorizo* rings, cut into large pieces
250g cherry tomatoes on the vine
2 heaped tablespoons marjoram or oregano leaves
80g baby spinach leaves
paprika dressing
2 teaspoons smoked paprika*
2 generous tablespoons maple syrup
2 generous tablespoons red wine vinegar

Preheat oven to 200°C (400°F). To make the paprika dressing, whisk together the paprika, maple and vinegar. Set aside.
    Place the squash and shallots on a baking tray lined with non-stick baking paper and drizzle with the oil. Roast for 25 minutes, add the chorizo, tomato and marjoram to the tray and roast for a further 15 minutes or until the squash is soft and the chorizo is golden and crisp.
    Place the spinach, tomato, squash, chorizo, shallots and pan juices in a bowl with the dressing and toss gently to combine. Divide between plates to serve. SERVES 4

crispy sesame-crusted tofu

caramelised chilli AND salmon stir-fry

asian duck AND cabbage salad

caramelised chilli AND salmon stir-fry

4 large red chillies, seeds removed and shredded
8 kaffir lime leaves*, finely shredded
1 heaped tablespoon grated ginger
125ml white vinegar
1 generous tablespoon fish sauce*
75g white sugar
500g salmon fillet, skin removed and thickly sliced
400g mange tout, blanched and shredded
30g coriander leaves
steamed rice or noodles, to serve

Place the chilli, lime leaves, ginger, vinegar, fish sauce and sugar in a large non-stick frying pan over high heat. Bring to the boil and cook for 3 minutes or until the mixture has thickened slightly. Add the salmon and cook for 1–2 minutes each side or until salmon is just cooked. Divide the mange tout and coriander between plates, top with the salmon and spoon over the pan sauce. Serve with steamed rice or noodles. SERVES 4

This versatile kale pesto is just as delicious on a sandwich as it is in a salad dressing.

asian duck AND cabbage salad

80ml lime juice
60ml fish sauce*
2 heaped tablespoons brown sugar
2 heaped tablespoons shredded ginger
6 kaffir lime leaves*, shredded
400g sliced store-bought Chinese roasted duck*
cabbage salad
240g white cabbage, finely shredded
2 large red chillies, shredded
3 spring onions, finely sliced
15g coriander leaves
10g mint leaves
15g basil leaves
50g roasted salted cashews

Place the lime juice, fish sauce, sugar, ginger and lime leaves in a large frying pan over low heat and bring to a simmer. Add the duck and toss to coat. Remove from the heat and set aside.

To make the cabbage salad, combine the cabbage, chilli, onion, coriander, mint and basil and divide between plates. Top with the duck and spoon over the pan sauce. Sprinkle with the cashews to serve. SERVES 4

kale AND cashew pesto pasta

400g spaghetti
kale and cashew pesto
300g kale, stems removed
10g flat-leaf parsley leaves
1 clove garlic, crushed
100g roasted salted cashews
2 teaspoons finely grated lemon rind
40g Parmesan, grated, plus extra, to serve
125ml extra virgin olive oil
lemon wedges, to serve

Cook the pasta in a large saucepan of salted boiling water for 8–10 minutes or until al dente. Drain and set aside.

While the pasta is cooking, place the kale and parsley in a food processor and pulse until finely chopped. Add the garlic, cashews, lemon rind, parmesan and oil and pulse until finely chopped and combined. Toss the pesto through the hot pasta and serve with the extra parmesan and lemon wedges. SERVES 4

kale AND cashew pesto pasta

sage AND garlic brined chicken

sage AND garlic brined chicken

1 litre cold water
85g table salt
8 sprigs sage
4 cloves garlic, smashed
4 x 160g chicken breast fillets, trimmed
30g unsalted butter
1 generous tablespoon extra virgin olive oil

Place the water and salt in a bowl and stir to dissolve. Add the sage, garlic and chicken and allow to stand for 15 minutes.

Remove the chicken, sage and garlic and pat dry with absorbent paper. Heat the butter and oil in a large non-stick frying pan over medium heat. Add the chicken and cook for 5 minutes. Add the sage and garlic, turn the chicken, and cook for a further 5 minutes or until the chicken is golden brown. Reduce the heat to low and cover the pan with a lid. Cook for 4 minutes, remove from the heat and stand, covered, for 2 minutes. Serve the chicken with the sage, garlic and pan juices. SERVES 4

RE-STYLE

SALAD BOWL *make it lunch*
Brush slices of prosciutto with maple syrup and bake until crisp. Slice the chicken and toss with rocket, cherry tomatoes and the prosciutto. Use the pan juices as a dressing and serve with aïoli*.

QUICK PASTA *friday dinner*
Cook store-bought cheese-filled ravioli and top with thin slices of the chicken. Spoon over the pan juices and sprinkle with finely grated parmesan, shredded lemon zest and crispy sage to serve.

crispy thai salmon cakes <u>with</u> chilli lime mayonnaise

green curry chicken stir-fry

crispy thai salmon cakes
WITH chilli lime mayonnaise

900g salmon fillet, skin removed
2 heaped tablespoons finely grated lime zest
2 heaped tablespoons finely grated ginger
2 large red chillies, seeds removed and finely sliced
10g coriander leaves
6 kaffir lime leaves*, shredded
1 generous tablespoon fish sauce*
2 egg whites
25g desiccated coconut*, lightly toasted
75g panko (Japanese) breadcrumbs*
vegetable oil, for brushing
chilli lime mayonnaise
225g whole-egg mayonnaise
2 large red chillies, seeds removed and finely chopped
60ml lime juice

To make the chilli lime mayonnaise, place the mayonnaise, chilli and lime juice in a bowl and mix to combine. Set aside.

   Chop the salmon into 2cm pieces. Place in a bowl with the lime zest, ginger, chilli, coriander, lime leaves, fish sauce, egg white, coconut and breadcrumbs and mix to combine. Shape 125ml portions of the mixture into patties. Place the patties on a large greased baking tray and brush with a little oil. Place under a preheated hot grill and cook for 2 minutes each side or until golden. Serve the fish cakes with the chilli lime mayonnaise and a simple cucumber salad, if desired. SERVES 4

green curry chicken stir-fry

3 x 160g chicken breast fillets, sliced
2 heaped tablespoons store-bought Thai green curry paste*
1 white onion, cut into thin wedges
2 generous tablespoons vegetable oil
2 teaspoons fish sauce*
1 heaped tablespoon palm sugar*
250ml coconut cream*
125ml chicken stock
2 generous tablespoons lime juice
200g green beans, trimmed
200g sugar snap peas, trimmed
4 kaffir lime leaves*, shredded
75g roasted salted cashews, chopped
coriander leaves, to serve
steamed jasmine rice or rice noodles, to serve

Place the chicken, curry paste and onion in a bowl and toss to combine. Heat the oil in a large non-stick frying pan or wok over high heat. Add the chicken and cook, stirring, for 4–5 minutes or until golden. Add the fish sauce, palm sugar, coconut cream, stock, lime juice, beans and sugar snap peas and cook, tossing, for a further 1–2 minutes or until the vegetables are tender. Top with the lime leaves, cashews and coriander and serve with noodles or rice. SERVES 4

green tea noodles
WITH dashi AND ginger tofu

200g green tea noodles*
dashi and ginger tofu
500g silken tofu*, sliced
750ml hot instant dashi broth*
½ cucumber, peeled and finely sliced
15g pickled ginger*, sliced
2 spring onions, finely chopped
baby coriander leaves, to serve
toasted sesame seeds and shichimi togarashi*, to serve

Cook the noodles in a large saucepan of salted boiling water until soft. Drain and divide the noodles between bowls. Top the noodles with the tofu, pour over the hot dashi broth and top with the cucumber, ginger, spring onion and coriander. Serve with the sesame seeds and shichimi togarashi. SERVES 4

green tea noodles WITH dashi AND ginger tofu

WEEKENDS

*These are the recipes I like to cook for family and friends
on the weekend, when things are a little more relaxed.
Whether it's a chic dinner or casual Sunday lunch, you'll find
inspiration for slow-cooked classics and easy-to-assemble feasts.*

juiciest roasted pork WITH salt AND pepper crackle

cashew chicken satay skewers

juiciest roasted pork WITH salt AND pepper crackle

1 x 1.2kg boneless pork loin, skin on
1 teaspoon fennel seeds, lightly crushed
2 heaped tablespoons sea salt flakes
1 heaped tablespoon cracked black pepper
2 teaspoons vegetable oil, plus extra, for brushing
sea salt, extra
1 bunch sage
2 small red apples, halved
60ml maple syrup
cracked black pepper, extra

Preheat oven to 220°C (425°F). Using a sharp knife, carefully remove the pork skin from the meat and trim both of any excess fat. Dry the skin well with absorbent paper. Place the fennel, salt, pepper and oil in a bowl and mix to combine. Place the pork skin on a baking tray lined with non-stick baking paper. Using a small, sharp knife, score the skin at 1cm intervals. Rub with half of the salt mixture. Roast for 5 minutes, reduce the temperature to 200°C (400°F) and roast for a further 18–20 minutes.

While the crackle is roasting, secure the pork with kitchen string, brush with the extra oil and rub with the remaining salt mixture. Heat a roasting pan on a hob over high heat. Add the pork and cook for 5 minutes each side or until well browned. Combine the apples and maple syrup and toss to coat. Place the sage under and around the pork and add the apples to the pan. Transfer to the oven and roast for 25–30 minutes for medium or until cooked to your liking. Cover and allow to rest for 10 minutes.

Slice the pork and divide between plates with the apples and sage. Cut the crackle into strips and serve with the pork. SERVES 4

cashew chicken satay skewers

180ml coconut cream*
225g roasted salted cashews
2 large red chillies, roughly chopped
2 cloves garlic, crushed
80ml soy sauce
800g chicken thigh fillets, cut into large pieces
125ml water
steamed jasmine rice, sesame seeds and baby coriander
   leaves, to serve

Place the coconut cream, cashews, chilli, garlic and soy in a food processor and process until a rough paste forms. Place half the cashew mixture in a bowl with the chicken and toss to coat. Thread the chicken onto skewers and place on a greased wire rack.

Cook under a preheated hot grill for 8–10 minutes each side or until golden and cooked through.

Place the remaining cashew mixture and the water in a saucepan over medium-high heat and bring to the boil. Cook for 2–3 minutes or until thickened. Sprinkle the rice with the sesame seeds and serve with the skewers, coriander and cashew sauce. SERVES 4

balsamic AND chorizo beef burgers

35g fresh breadcrumbs
2 generous tablespoons milk
½ dried chorizo* ring, skin removed and chopped
400g beef mince
2 generous tablespoons balsamic glaze*
1 heaped tablespoon chopped oregano leaves
sea salt and cracked black pepper
1 small (230g) aubergine, thinly sliced
extra virgin olive oil, for brushing
4 bread rolls, halved
store-bought aïoli* and rocket leaves, to serve

Place the breadcrumbs in a bowl, pour over the milk and allow to stand for 5 minutes. Place the chorizo in a food processor and process until finely chopped. Transfer to a large bowl with the mince, balsamic, oregano, breadcrumb mixture, salt and pepper and mix to combine.

Preheat a barbecue or char-grill pan over medium heat. Shape the mixture into 4 even-sized patties and cook for 3 minutes each side or until cooked through. Set aside. Brush the aubergine with a little oil and cook for 2 minutes each side.

To assemble, spread the bottoms of the buns with the aïoli, top with rocket, a beef patty and the aubergine. Sandwich with the tops of the buns to serve. SERVES 4

balsamic AND chorizo beef burgers

basil AND ricotta gnocchi WITH roasted tomatoes

spicy chicken laksa

basil AND ricotta gnocchi WITH roasted tomatoes

500g fresh ricotta
30g shredded basil leaves
60g Parmesan, grated
2 eggs, lightly beaten
150g plain flour
½ teaspoon sea salt flakes
60g butter
basil and rocket leaves, to serve
roasted tomatoes
600g mixed cherry tomatoes, halved
2 heaped tablespoons oregano leaves
12 cloves garlic, unpeeled
60ml extra virgin olive oil
60ml red wine vinegar
1 heaped tablespoon caster sugar
sea salt and cracked black pepper

Preheat oven to 200°C (400°F). To make the roasted tomatoes, place the tomatoes, oregano and garlic on a baking tray lined with non-stick baking paper. Combine the oil, vinegar, sugar, salt and pepper and pour half the mixture over the tomatoes. Roast for 15 minutes or until the tomatoes and garlic are soft and golden. Set aside.

Place the ricotta, basil, parmesan, egg, flour and salt in a bowl and mix until a soft dough forms. Transfer to a lightly floured surface and using lightly floured hands, take 2 teaspoons of dough at a time and shape into small flat dumplings. Place on a sheet of non-stick baking paper.

Cook the gnocchi, in batches, in a large saucepan of salted boiling water for 2–3 minutes or until the gnocchi float to the surface. Drain and set aside.

Melt half the butter in a large non-stick frying pan over high heat. Add half the gnocchi and cook for 3 minutes each side or until golden. Repeat with remaining butter and gnocchi.

Divide the gnocchi between plates with the roasted tomatoes and garlic. Spoon over the pan juices and remaining dressing and sprinkle with the basil. Serve with the rocket. **SERVES 4**

spicy chicken laksa

2 x 160g chicken breast fillets, trimmed and thinly sliced
2 heaped tablespoons Asian chilli jam*
1 generous tablespoon vegetable oil
2 heaped tablespoons store-bought laksa paste*
500ml chicken stock
1 generous tablespoon fish sauce*
2 kaffir lime leaves*
1 x 400ml tin coconut milk*
200g rice vermicelli*
250g bean sprouts
15g coriander leaves
25g Thai or ordinary basil leaves
lime wedges, to serve

Place the chicken and chilli jam in a bowl and toss to coat. Heat the oil in a large deep frying pan over high heat. Add the chicken and cook, turning, for 2–3 minutes or until golden. Set aside and keep warm.

Add the laksa paste to the pan and cook for 1 minute. Return the chicken to the pan with the stock, fish sauce, kaffir lime and coconut milk and bring to the boil. Cook for 2–3 minutes or until thickened.

Place the noodles in a bowl, cover with boiling water and allow to stand for 5 minutes or until tender. Drain the noodles and divide between bowls. Divide the broth between the bowls and serve with the chicken, bean sprouts, coriander, Thai basil and lime. **SERVES 4**

crispy chicken wings

1kg chicken wings
35g cornflour
2 generous tablespoons vegetable oil
1 heaped tablespoon sea salt flakes
½ teaspoon Chinese five-spice powder*
1 teaspoon dried chilli flakes
hot chilli sauce, pickled chilli, thinly sliced fresh chilli and
    chilli mayonnaise (optional), to serve

Preheat oven to 220°C (425°F). Using kitchen scissors, trim the tips from the wings and discard. Cut the wings in half at the joint and place in a plastic bag with the cornflour. Shake to coat, dusting off any excess cornflour.

Place the oil, salt, five-spice and dried chilli in a large bowl. Add the wings and toss to coat. Place on a baking tray lined with non-stick baking paper and roast for 25–30 minutes or until crisp. Serve with chilli sauce, chillies and chilli mayonnaise. **SERVES 4**

crispy chicken wings

caramelised onion AND olive roasted lamb

caramelised onion AND olive roasted lamb

6 sprigs rosemary
1 x 1kg lamb leg, boned, flattened and trimmed[+]
sea salt and cracked black pepper
340g store-bought caramelised onion relish*
75g pitted olives, crushed
1 heaped tablespoon rosemary leaves, extra
5 anchovy fillets, roughly chopped
1 generous tablespoon extra virgin olive oil

Preheat oven to 240°C (475°F). Place the rosemary sprigs in the base of a baking dish lined with non-stick baking paper. Top with the lamb and sprinkle well with salt and pepper. Combine the onion, olives, extra rosemary, anchovy and oil. Score the lamb and spread with the onion mixture. Roast for 10 minutes, reduce the temperature to 180°C (350°F) and cook for a further 10–15 minutes or until the lamb is cooked to your liking. Slice the lamb thickly to serve. SERVES 4
+ Ask your butcher to bone the lamb leg for you.

RE-STYLE

CASUAL SUNDAY *wrap it up*
Slice the lamb and serve with store-bought flatbread, dips such as baba ghanoush or hummus, and tabbouli.

SUMMER SALAD *make it fresh*
Slice the lamb and serve with a salad of heirloom or vine tomatoes, oregano leaves and a drizzle of extra virgin olive oil.

ribs <u>WITH</u> chipotle-maple barbecue sauce

cheat's spinach, ricotta AND squash lasagne

porchetta

ribs WITH chipotle-maple barbecue sauce

1.2kg American-style rack of
   pork ribs
1 onion, quartered
2 cloves garlic, halved
6 sprigs thyme
chipotle-maple barbecue sauce
280g tomato passata
80ml maple syrup
60ml malt vinegar
2 heaped tablespoons mustard powder
2 chipotle chillies, dried and rehydrated
   or in adobo sauce*, chopped

Preheat oven to 200°C (400°F). To make the chipotle-maple
barbecue sauce, place the tomato, maple, vinegar, mustard
and chilli in a small saucepan over medium heat. Cook, stirring,
for 8–10 minutes or until thickened. Set aside.
   Cut the ribs into large sections and place in a large saucepan
with the onion, garlic and thyme. Add enough cold water to
cover the ribs, place over high heat and bring to the boil.
Reduce the heat to low and simmer for 25 minutes. Drain the
ribs, discarding the onion, garlic and thyme.
   Transfer the ribs to two baking trays lined with non-stick baking
paper. Generously brush the sauce over both sides of the ribs.
Roast for 15 minutes, brush with more sauce and roast for
a further 15 minutes or until the ribs are golden. Serve with the
remaining sauce and potato fries, if desired. SERVES 4

cheat's spinach, ricotta AND squash lasagne

750g store-bought spinach and ricotta ravioli
500g frozen spinach, thawed
440g grated butternut squash
560g tomato passata
15g chopped basil leaves
sea salt and cracked black pepper
750g fresh ricotta
100g mozzarella, grated
2 heaped tablespoons oregano leaves
20g Parmesan, grated

Preheat oven to 180°C (350°F). Cook the ravioli in a saucepan
of boiling salted water for 3 minutes or until half cooked. Drain and
layer half the ravioli in the base of a lightly greased 3.5-litre-
capacity ovenproof dish. Squeeze the excess liquid from the spinach
and spread half over the ravioli. Top with half the ricotta. Combine
the squash, tomato, basil, salt and pepper and spread half over the
ricotta. Repeat with another layer of pasta, spinach and squash,
finishing with a layer of ricotta. Sprinkle with the mozzarella,
oregano and Parmesan. Cover with non-stick baking paper and
aluminium foil and bake for 1 hour 20 minutes. Uncover and cook
for a further 35 minutes or until golden. SERVES 8–10

porchetta

2 heaped tablespoons fennel seeds
2 heaped tablespoons rosemary leaves
2 heaped tablespoons marjoram or oregano leaves
1 heaped tablespoon finely grated lemon zest
2 heaped tablespoons caster sugar
1 heaped tablespoon sea salt flakes
1 teaspoon cracked black pepper
3kg boneless pork loin, belly piece attached, skin on

Place the fennel seeds in a small food processor and process
until finely ground. Add the rosemary, marjoram, lemon, sugar,
salt and pepper, and process until finely chopped.
   Using a meat tenderiser, pound the pork skin for 3 minutes,
then score the skin at 1cm intervals. Turn the pork and spread
the herb mixture on the meaty side. Refrigerate, skin-side up,
on a baking tray lined with non-stick baking paper for at least
2 hours or overnight.
   Preheat oven to 250°C (475°F). Tuck the pork under itself and
tie loosely with kitchen string. Roast for 30–35 minutes or until
the skin has crackled. Reduce the heat to 120°C (250°F) and
roast for a further 2 hours or until the pork is just cooked through.
Thinly slice the pork to serve. SERVE 6–8

balsamic beef short ribs

crispy duck <u>with</u> ginger plums

balsamic beef short ribs

1.6kg beef short ribs
sea salt and cracked black pepper
2 red onions, cut into wedges
8 cloves garlic, peeled
6 sprigs oregano
375ml balsamic vinegar
1 x 400g tin chopped tomatoes
1 litre beef stock
basil gremolata
50g small basil leaves
1 heaped tablespoon finely grated lemon zest
1 clove garlic, crushed
1 teaspoon extra virgin olive oil

To make the basil gremolata, place the basil, lemon, garlic, oil, salt and pepper in a bowl and mix to combine. Set aside.

Heat a large, deep heavy-based casserole dish over medium-high heat. Sprinkle the ribs with salt and pepper and cook for 4–5 minutes each side or until well browned. Remove from the dish and set aside.

Wipe the dish with absorbent paper, add the onion and garlic and cook for 5 minutes or until golden. Return the ribs to the dish with the oregano, vinegar, tomato, stock, salt and pepper, reduce the heat to low, cover and simmer for 2½–3 hours or until the beef is very tender. Remove the ribs from the dish and keep warm.

Strain the pan juices and skim the fat from the surface. Pour into a saucepan and simmer over high heat for 5–10 minutes or until the sauce has thickened. Divide the ribs between plates and spoon over the sauce. Sprinkle over the gremolata to serve. **SERVES 4**

crispy duck WITH ginger plums

4 x 250g duck legs with thigh, trimmed
sea salt and cracked black pepper
5g small sage leaves
2 teaspoons juniper berries*, lightly crushed
ginger plums
35g shredded or chopped ginger
1 large red chilli, seeds removed and shredded
310ml ginger wine or ginger beer
2 heaped tablespoons brown sugar
6 plums, halved and stones removed

Preheat oven to 180°C (350°F). To make the ginger plums, place the ginger, chilli, ginger wine, sugar and plums, cut-side up, in a baking dish. Roast for 25 minutes, basting occasionally with the pan sauce, or until the plums are soft.

Heat a large non-stick frying pan over medium heat. Sprinkle the duck generously with salt and pepper and cook, skin-side down, for 10 minutes or until the skin is golden and crisp. Place the sage and juniper in a baking dish and top with the duck, skin-side up. Roast for 20 minutes or until tender. Divide the duck between plates and serve with sage and ginger plums. **SERVES 4**

the best roast chicken

150g table salt
3 litres water
1 x 1.5kg whole chicken
6 sprigs tarragon
1 lemon, sliced
1 head garlic, halved crossways
1 heaped tablespoon black peppercorns
extra virgin olive oil, for brushing
sea salt flakes
30g butter, melted

Place the salt and water in a large high-sided plastic container or glass bowl and stir to dissolve the salt. Add the chicken, tarragon, lemon, garlic and peppercorns, ensuring the chicken is fully submerged. Cover and refrigerate for a maximum of 4 hours. Drain the chicken and pat dry, reserving the tarragon, lemon and garlic.

Preheat oven to 180°C (350°F). Place the chicken in a baking dish. Fill the cavity with the reserved tarragon, garlic and lemon and secure the legs with kitchen string. Brush the chicken with oil, sprinkle with salt and roast for 1 hour. Brush the chicken with the melted butter and any pan juices and roast for a further 15–20 minutes or until golden and cooked through. **SERVES 4–6**

the best roast chicken

smoky pulled pork

smoky pulled pork

1 x 1.5kg boneless pork shoulder, rind removed
sea salt and cracked black pepper
1 generous tablespoon extra virgin olive oil
1 onion, finely diced
8 cloves garlic, peeled and halved
1 heaped tablespoon smoked paprika*
3 dried ancho* or large red chillies, halved
1 x 400g tin chopped tomatoes
125ml malt vinegar
125ml maple syrup
125ml bourbon whiskey
375ml beef stock
10 sprigs thyme
sea salt and cracked black pepper
soft bread rolls, avocado wedges, lime wedges, baby
  coriander leaves and barbecued corn, to serve

Preheat oven to 160°C (350°F). Trim the pork of any excess fat and sprinkle with salt and pepper. Heat a heavy-based ovenproof casserole dish on a hob over high heat. Add the oil and pork and cook for 5 minutes each side or until well browned. Remove from the dish and add the onion and garlic. Cook for 4 minutes or until light golden.

Return the pork to the dish and add the paprika, chilli, tomato, vinegar, maple syrup, bourbon, stock, thyme, salt and pepper and bring to a simmer. Cover, transfer to the oven and bake for 2½ hours, turning the pork halfway through the cooking time. Uncover and cook for a further 30 minutes or until the pork is very tender. Shred the pork using two forks and return to the pan juices. Serve the pork with the bread rolls, avocado, lime, coriander and corn. SERVES 6

RE-STYLE

DECONSTRUCTED *the new nachos*
Serve the pulled pork as part of a shared platter with its sides and crispy tortilla pieces for dipping.

MEXICAN FEAST *tasty tacos*
Chargrill soft tortillas until warmed through and serve with the pulled pork and its sides.

salt-marinated pork chops

slow-roasted pomegranate lamb shoulder

roasted cauliflower AND chickpea soup

salt-marinated pork chops

1 litre water
125g table salt
375ml chilled apple juice
8 sprigs sage
1 teaspoon juniper berries*, lightly crushed
1 cinnamon stick
4 cloves garlic, halved
2 x 450g double pork loin cutlets, skin scored
30g unsalted butter
1 generous tablespoon extra virgin olive oil
500ml dry apple cider*

Place 250ml water and the salt in a saucepan over medium heat and stir to dissolve. Remove from the heat and pour into a large 4-litre-capacity container. Add the remaining water, juice, sage, juniper, cinnamon and garlic. Add the pork, ensuring it's fully covered with liquid, and refrigerate for a maximum of 4 hours.
    Preheat oven to 200°C (400°F). Remove the pork from the brining liquid and pat dry. Remove the sage, garlic, juniper and cinnamon and set aside. Heat the butter and oil in a large heavy-based ovenproof casserole dish over medium-high heat. Add the pork and cook for 4–6 minutes each side or until well browned. Add the reserved sage, garlic, juniper, cinnamon and cider and transfer to the oven. Roast for 20–30 minutes or until the pork is cooked to your liking. Serve the pork with the pan sauce. SERVES 4

slow-roasted pomegranate lamb shoulder

1 x 2kg lamb shoulder, bone in, trimmed of excess fat
6 cloves garlic, peeled and halved
1 heaped tablespoon ras el hanout*
2 heaped tablespoons oregano leaves
1 x 400g tin chopped tomatoes
375ml beef stock
2 generous tablespoons pomegranate molasses*, plus extra,
  to serve
sea salt and cracked black pepper
currants and cooked couscous, to serve
5g flat-leaf parsley leaves
40g pine nuts, toasted

Preheat oven to 170°C (350°F). Place the lamb, garlic, ras el hanout, oregano, tomato, stock, molasses, salt and pepper in a baking dish. Cover and bake for 3 hours, turning the lamb halfway through. Uncover and cook, meaty side up, for a further 30 minutes. Remove the bone and transfer the lamb to a serving dish. Spoon over the pan juices, drizzle with the extra molasses and serve with couscous, currants, parsley and pine nuts. SERVES 4

roasted cauliflower AND chickpea soup

1 x 1kg cauliflower, trimmed and cut into small florets
1 x 400g tin chickpeas, rinsed and drained
4 cloves garlic, peeled
4 sprigs thyme
1 heaped tablespoon shredded lemon zest
1 teaspoon ground cumin
60ml extra virgin olive oil
sea salt and cracked black pepper
1 potato, peeled and finely chopped
1.5 litres chicken stock
1 teaspoon sumac*
plain yoghurt, to serve

Preheat oven to 200°C (400°F). Divide the cauliflower, chickpeas, garlic, thyme and lemon between 2 baking trays lined with non-stick paper. Sprinkle with the cumin, salt and pepper, drizzle with the oil and roast for 25–30 minutes or until golden.
    Place the potato and chicken stock in a large saucepan and bring to the boil over high heat. Simmer for 8 minutes or until the potato is tender. Add half the cauliflower and chickpeas and cook for 1–2 minutes or until tender. Using a hand-held stick blender, purée until smooth. Divide the soup between bowls and top with the remaining cauliflower and chickpeas. Sprinkle with the sumac and serve with yoghurt. SERVES 4

roasted garlic AND harissa lamb shoulder

quinoa, kale AND preserved lemon fritters

chicken AND mushroom pies

roasted garlic AND harissa lamb shoulder

2 heaped tablespoons harissa paste*
3 shallots, finely chopped
15g coriander leaves, finely chopped
2 generous tablespoons extra virgin olive oil
2 heaped tablespoons finely chopped preserved lemon rind*
1 x 2kg lamb shoulder, trimmed
sea salt and cracked black pepper
extra virgin olive oil, extra, for drizzling
2 heads garlic, halved crossways
2 heaped tablespoons store-bought dukkah*
280g plain yoghurt
mint leaves, rocket leaves and charred lemon wedges, to serve

Preheat oven to 160°C (325°F). Place the harissa, shallots, coriander, oil and preserved lemon in a bowl and mix to combine. Place the lamb shoulder in a baking dish and spread evenly with the harissa mixture. Sprinkle with salt and pepper and drizzle with a little oil. Place the garlic and 125ml of water in the base of the baking dish, cover with aluminium foil and roast for 3½ hours. Remove the foil and cook for a further 30–40 minutes, basting occasionally with the pan juices, or until the lamb is tender and the sauce has thickened. Transfer the lamb and garlic to a large platter and spoon over the remaining pan juices. Sprinkle with the dukkah and serve with the yoghurt, mint, rocket and lemon. SERVES 6

quinoa, kale AND preserved lemon fritters

760g cooked white quinoa*
4 eggs
250g fresh ricotta
2 heaped tablespoons finely chopped preserved lemon rind*
6 stalks kale, stems removed and shredded
15g finely chopped flat-leaf parsley leaves
sea salt and cracked black pepper
extra virgin olive oil, for frying
200g store-bought tzatziki
small flat-leaf parsley leaves, sumac* and lemon wedges, to serve

Place the quinoa, eggs and ricotta in a bowl and mix well to combine. Add the preserved lemon, kale, parsley, salt and pepper and mix well to combine. Heat a little of the oil in large non-stick frying pan over medium heat. Shape 3–4 tablespoons of mixture into patties and cook, in batches, for 3–4 minutes each side or until the fritters are golden and crisp. Set aside and keep warm.

Divide the fritters between plates and serve with the tzatziki, parsley, sumac and lemon wedges. SERVE 4

chicken AND mushroom pies

50g unsalted butter
250g chestnut mushrooms, sliced
4 cloves garlic, sliced
1 teaspoon juniper berries*, chopped
5g tarragon leaves
1 heaped tablespoon finely grated orange zest
3 heaped tablespoons plain flour
375ml chicken stock
480g cooked chicken, chopped
1 egg, lightly beaten
hot water pastry
225g unsalted butter
500ml water
675g plain flour
2 teaspoons sea salt flakes

Melt the butter in a large non-stick frying pan over medium heat. Add the mushrooms, garlic and juniper and cook, stirring, for 2–3 minutes or until golden. Add the tarragon and orange zest and cook for a further minute. Add the flour to the pan and cook, stirring, for another 1–2 minutes. Add the stock and chicken and cook, stirring, until the sauce begins to thicken. Discard the juniper berries and set aside to cool completely.

To make the hot water pastry, place the butter and water in a small saucepan and bring to the boil. Place the flour and salt in a bowl and pour over the hot water mixture, mixing with a butter knife to combine. Turn out onto a lightly floured surface and bring the dough together to form a ball. Allow to cool slightly.

Roll the dough out on a lightly floured surface to 5mm thick and using a plate as a guide, cut 4 x 20cm rounds for the base of the pies and 4 x 9cm rounds for the tops. Place the large rounds in the base of 4 lightly greased 500ml-capacity tall pie tins and fill with the chicken mixture. Brush the edges with egg and top with the small pastry rounds. Press the edges together to seal and make a small slit in the top of each pie. Brush with the remaining egg and bake for 30–35 minutes or until golden. MAKES 8

slow-cooked brisket

slow-cooked brisket

1 x 2kg beef brisket, trimmed
sea salt and cracked black pepper
2 generous tablespoons extra virgin olive oil
150g diced pancetta*
1 onion, finely diced
4 cloves garlic, crushed
375ml red wine
125ml red wine vinegar
2 heaped tablespoons brown sugar
2 x 400g tins chopped tomatoes
500ml beef stock
375ml water
2 bay leaves
3 sprigs rosemary

Preheat oven to 180°C (350°F). Sprinkle the meat with salt and pepper. Heat the oil in a large heavy-based ovenproof casserole dish over high heat and cook for 2–3 minutes each side or until well browned. Set aside.

Add the pancetta to the dish and cook, stirring, for 3 minutes. Add the onion and garlic and cook for a further 2 minutes or until golden. Return the beef to the dish with the wine, vinegar, brown sugar, tomato, stock, water, bay leaves and rosemary.

Cover and cook for 3½–4 hours, turning halfway through the cooking time, or until tender. Using 2 forks, shred the meat and serve with the pan sauce. **SERVES 6**

RE-STYLE

INDULGENT DINNER *in a lasagne*
Blanch long sheets of fresh lasagne and place on baking trays lined with non-stick baking paper. Fold the lasagne sheets in on themselves, placing brisket and mozzarella between the layers. Bake for 15 minutes and sprinkle with parmesan and basil to serve.

PURE COMFORT *warming bowls*
For a warming meal, serve the brisket with bowls of creamy polenta. Sprinkle with finely grated parmesan and basil.

spiced lamb AND quince meatballs

lamb shanks rogan josh

spiced lamb AND quince meatballs

70g fresh breadcrumbs
60ml milk
750g lamb mince
2 heaped tablespoons quince paste*, softened
1 clove garlic, crushed
1 teaspoon ground cumin
2 teaspoons chopped rosemary
sea salt and cracked black pepper
extra virgin olive oil, for frying
30g coriander leaves
170g pomegranate seeds
shredded courgette and mint leaves, to serve
yoghurt dressing
140g plain yoghurt
2 generous tablespoons lemon juice
70g tahini paste*
2–3 generous tablespoons water

Preheat oven to 180°C (350°F). To make the yoghurt dressing, place the yoghurt, lemon and tahini in a bowl and whisk to combine. Slowly add the water, whisking until the dressing is the consistency of thick cream. Set aside.

Place the breadcrumbs and milk in a bowl and allow to soak for 4 minutes. Add the lamb, quince, garlic, cumin, rosemary, salt and pepper and mix well to combine. Shape 3–4 tablespoons of mixture into balls. Heat a little of the oil in a large non-stick frying pan over medium-high heat. Cook the meatballs, in batches, for 1–2 minutes each side or until well browned. Transfer to a baking tray lined with non-stick baking paper. Bake the meatballs for 8–10 minutes or until just cooked through.

Divide the meatballs between plates and serve with the yoghurt dressing, courgette, mint, pomegranate and coriander. SERVES 4

lamb shanks rogan josh

2 generous tablespoons extra virgin olive oil
2 onions, chopped
4 cloves garlic, crushed
4 x 250g lamb shanks
sea salt and cracked black pepper
150g store-bought rogan josh curry paste
2 x 400g tins chopped tomatoes
1 x 400ml tin coconut milk*
500ml chicken stock
2 heaped tablespoons tomato paste
store-bought tzatziki, mint leaves and coriander leaves, to serve

Preheat oven to 180°C (350°F). Heat the oil in a large non-stick frying pan over medium heat, add the onions and garlic and cook for 5–7 minutes or until soft. Transfer to a large deep-sided roasting dish. Sprinkle the lamb with salt and pepper and cook, turning, for 2–3 minutes each side or until well browned. Transfer to the roasting dish with the curry paste, tomato, coconut milk, stock and tomato paste. Mix to combine, cover with aluminium foil and cook for 3 hours, turning halfway. Remove the foil and cook for a further 30 minutes or until the sauce has thickened. Serve the lamb with the tzatziki, mint and coriander. SERVES 4

spicy sausage rolls

500g pork mince
150g speck*, finely chopped
2 heaped tablespoons harissa paste*
1½ tablespoons honey
2 heaped tablespoons thyme leaves, plus extra sprigs,
  to decorate
sea salt and cracked black pepper
320g store-bought puff pastry sheets, thawed and cut into
  2 sheets
1 egg, lightly beaten
caramelised onion relish* and tomato chutney, to serve

Preheat oven to 200°C (400°F). Place the mince, speck, harissa, honey and thyme in a bowl and mix until well combined. Place the mince mixture along the long side of each pastry sheet, brush with egg and roll to enclose. Trim the sides and brush the tops with egg. Make six cuts in the tops of the sausage rolls and place thyme sprigs in the cuts. Bake for 35 minutes or until golden. Serve with caramelised onion relish and tomato chutney. SERVES 4

spicy sausage rolls

sloppy joe sliders

pork AND prawn potsticker dumplings

prawn dumpling soup

sloppy joe sliders

1 generous tablespoon extra virgin olive oil
1 onion, chopped
2 cloves garlic, crushed
500g minced beef
560g tomato passata*
1 heaped tablespoon Dijon mustard
60ml apple cider vinegar
1 heaped tablespoon brown sugar
sea salt and cracked black pepper
1 x 400g tin black beans, drained and rinsed
8 small soft bread rolls
lettuce leaves and sour cream, to serve

Heat a large non-stick frying pan over medium-high heat. Add the oil, onion and garlic and cook for 5 minutes or until golden. Add the mince and cook, breaking up any lumps with a wooden spoon, for 10 minutes or until lightly browned. Add the tomato, mustard, vinegar, sugar, salt and pepper and simmer for 5–7 minutes or until the mixture has thickened. Stir through the beans and cook for a further 2 minutes or until warmed through. Halve the rolls and top with the lettuce, beef mixture and sour cream to serve. SERVES 4

pork AND prawn potsticker dumplings

12 large raw prawns, peeled and cleaned
200g fine pork mince
2 teaspoons grated ginger
1 small red chilli, finely chopped
1 heaped tablespoon Asian chilli jam*
1 generous tablespoon soy sauce
1 spring onion, finely chopped
25 round wonton wrappers*
2 generous tablespoons vegetable oil
250ml chicken stock
250ml water
soy, chilli sauce and sliced fresh chilli, to serve

Cut the prawns into chunks and place in a bowl with the pork, ginger, chilli, chilli jam, soy and onion. Mix well to combine. Place 1½ teaspoons of the mixture onto half of each wonton. Brush the edges with water and fold to enclose the filling. Press the edges to seal and repeat with remaining wontons. Heat a non-stick frying pan over medium-high heat. Add half the oil, half the stock and half the water and bring to the boil. Add half the dumplings and cook, covered, for 5 minutes. Remove the lid and cook for a further 3–4 minutes or until the bases are crisp. Repeat with remaining dumplings. Serve with soy, chilli sauce and chilli. SERVES 4

prawn dumpling soup

12 large raw prawns, peeled and finely chopped
2 teaspoons grated ginger
½ teaspoon sesame oil
1 spring onion, finely chopped
20 round wonton wrappers*
soup
1 litre chicken stock
1 generous tablespoon soy sauce
60ml Chinese cooking wine (Shaoxing)*
6 slices ginger
2 generous tablespoons lime juice
500ml water
2 bok choy*, sliced
2 kaffir lime leaves*, finely sliced
3 spring onions, finely sliced
sliced green chilli and lime wedges, to serve

Place the prawns, ginger, sesame oil and green onion in a bowl and mix to combine. Place 1 teaspoon of the mixture into the centre of each wonton wrapper, brush the edges with water and fold to enclose. Pinch the edges together to seal and fold over the ends to meet. Set aside.

To make the soup, place the stock, soy, cooking wine, ginger, lime juice and water in a large saucepan over medium-high heat and bring to the boil. Add the dumplings and simmer for 4–6 minutes or until just cooked through. Add the bok choy and lime leaves. Divide the dumplings, bok choy and broth between bowls and serve with the spring onion, chilli and lime wedges. SERVES 4

lime AND tequila fish tacos

lime AND tequila fish tacos

60ml tequila
60ml lime juice
1 heaped tablespoon caster sugar
1 teaspoon dried chilli flakes
sea salt
8 small white fish fillets
vegetable oil, for brushing
8 tortillas, warmed
1 avocado, diced
15g coriander leaves
pickled cabbage salad
1 white onion, thinly sliced
160g cabbage, shredded

Mix to combine the tequila, lime, sugar, chilli and salt. Place the fish in a bowl, pour over half the tequila mixture and allow to stand for 20 minutes to marinate.

To make the pickled cabbage salad, place the onion and cabbage in a bowl and pour over the remaining tequila marinade. Toss to combine and refrigerate until required.

Remove the fish from the marinade and brush with a little oil. Heat a large non-stick frying pan or barbecue over high heat and cook the fish, skin-side first, for 1–2 minutes each side. Set aside.

To make the tacos, top the tortillas with the cabbage salad, avocado, fish and coriander. SERVES 4

RE-STYLE

TASTY BURGERS *saturday lunch*
Replace the tortillas with soft bread rolls. Mix a few teaspoons of the tequila marinade with a little mayonnaise to serve on the side.

SALAD DAYS *fresh and easy*
Arrange the ingredients on serving plates without the tortillas to make an elegant salad. Serve with lime wedges.

thai beef <u>with</u> spicy carrot salad

moroccan-spiced chicken

thai beef WITH spicy carrot salad

2 heaped tablespoons Asian chilli jam*
1 x 800g beef fillet
1 generous tablespoon vegetable oil
3 carrots, thinly sliced with a julienne peeler
¾ cucumber, peeled, halved and sliced lengthways
2 shallots, thinly sliced
15g baby coriander leaves
15g Thai or ordinary basil leaves
70g salted roasted peanuts, chopped
chilli dressing
2 heaped tablespoons Asian chilli jam*
1 heaped tablespoon palm sugar*, grated
1 generous tablespoon fish sauce*
2 generous tablespoons lime juice

To make the chilli dressing, place the chilli jam, palm sugar,
fish sauce and lime juice in a small food processor and process
until combined. Set aside.

Rub the chilli jam over the beef fillet. Heat the oil in a large
non-stick frying pan over medium heat and cook the beef, turning,
for 6–8 minutes each side or until browned and medium-rare.
Place the carrot, cucumber, shallots, coriander and basil in
a bowl, pour over a little of the dressing and toss to combine. Slice
the beef and serve with the carrot salad, peanuts and remaining
dressing. SERVES 4

moroccan-spiced chicken

1 x 1.5kg whole chicken, quartered
1 heaped tablespoon ras el hanout*
2 heaped tablespoons sliced preserved lemon rind*
2 generous tablespoons extra virgin olive oil
10 sprigs oregano
1 red onion, cut into wedges
4 parsnips, peeled and cut into sixths lengthways
sea salt

Preheat oven to 200°C (400°F). Place the chicken, ras el hanout,
lemon and 1 tablespoon of the oil in a bowl and toss to coat.
Transfer to a baking dish lined with non-stick baking paper with
the oregano, onion and parsnips and drizzle with the remaining oil.
Sprinkle with salt and roast for 35–45 minutes or until the chicken
is golden and cooked through. Divide the chicken, onion and parsnip
between plates and spoon over the pan juices to serve. SERVES 4

crab pasta WITH oven-roasted cherry tomatoes

400g cherry tomatoes, halved
1 generous tablespoon extra virgin olive oil
1 teaspoon caster sugar
sea salt and cracked black pepper
400g capellini (angel hair) pasta
50g unsalted butter
1 teaspoon dried chilli flakes
3 cloves garlic, crushed
1 heaped tablespoon shredded lemon zest
800ml chicken stock
2 generous tablespoons lemon juice
500g crab meat, picked+
baby basil leaves and lemon wedges, to serve

Preheat oven to 180°C (350°F). Place the tomatoes on a
baking tray lined with non-stick baking paper, drizzle with
the oil and sprinkle with the sugar, salt and pepper. Roast for
20 minutes or until caramelised.

Cook the pasta in a large pot of boiling salted water for
3–4 minutes or until al dente. Drain and set aside.

Melt the butter in a large non-stick frying pan over medium
heat. Add the chilli, garlic and lemon zest and cook, stirring,
for 1 minute or until golden. Add the chicken stock and cook for
1–2 minutes or until the sauce has reduced. Add the pasta and
lemon juice and toss to combine. Divide between plates with the
tomatoes and top with the crab and basil leaves to serve. SERVES 4
+ You can buy fresh or frozen picked crab meat from your fishmonger.

crab pasta <u>with</u> oven-roasted cherry tomatoes

sticky korean pork <u>with</u> apple <small>AND</small> cucumber pickle

slow-roasted beef <u>with</u> leeks

sticky korean pork WITH apple AND cucumber pickle

80ml soy sauce
60ml mirin*
2 generous tablespoons rice wine vinegar
110g caster sugar
3 heaped tablespoons gochujang* (chilli paste)
2 cloves garlic, crushed
1 heaped tablespoon grated ginger
1 generous tablespoon vegetable oil
1 x 1kg pork neck fillet, trimmed and sliced
steamed jasmine rice and baby basil leaves, to serve
apple and cucumber pickle
½ cucumber, thinly sliced
1 Granny Smith apple, sliced into rounds
1 long red chilli, sliced
80ml rice wine vinegar
2 heaped tablespoons caster sugar

To make the apple and cucumber pickle, place the cucumber, apple, chilli, vinegar and sugar in a bowl, toss to combine and set aside.

Place the soy sauce, mirin, vinegar, sugar, chilli paste, garlic and ginger in a bowl and mix to combine. Add the pork and toss to coat. Thread the pork onto metal skewers and cook under a preheated hot grill for 5–7 minutes, or until cooked through. Serve the skewers with the apple and cucumber pickle, steamed rice and baby basil leaves. SERVES 4

slow-roasted beef WITH leeks

4 leeks, trimmed and halved lengthways
2 generous tablespoons extra virgin olive oil
1 x 1.6kg beef sirloin roast
1 generous tablespoon extra virgin olive oil, extra
400ml beef stock
sea salt and cracked black pepper
2 heaped tablespoons chopped tarragon
2 heaped tablespoons thyme leaves

Preheat oven to 100°C (212°F). Cover the leeks with boiling water and allow to stand for 5 minutes. Drain and pat dry. Place the leeks in the base of a baking tray, drizzle with the oil and pour over the beef stock.

Brush the beef with extra oil and generously sprinkle with salt and pepper. Heat a large non-stick frying pan over medium heat and cook the beef for 3 minutes each side or until just browned. Place the beef on top of the leeks and sprinkle with the tarragon and thyme leaves. Roast for 2 hours or until the leeks are tender and the beef is cooked to medium-rare. Remove the beef from pan, cover and keep warm.

Increase the oven temperature to 220°C (425°F) and cook the leeks for a further 10–15 minutes or until golden. Thinly slice the beef and serve with the leeks and pan juices. SERVES 6-8

sherry-roasted lamb

16 sprigs thyme
16 sprigs oregano
1 x 2.2kg lamb leg, trimmed
sea salt and cracked black pepper
500ml sweet sherry
2 generous tablespoons apple cider vinegar
250ml beef stock
2 heaped tablespoons brown sugar
1 teaspoon juniper berries*
12 cloves garlic, skin on
8 shallots, peeled

Preheat oven to 200°C (400°F). Tie the thyme and oregano around the lamb using kitchen string and sprinkle with salt and pepper. Place the sherry, vinegar, stock, sugar, juniper, garlic and shallots in a baking dish and top with the lamb. Roast for 20–30 minutes or until the lamb is golden. Turn, cook for a further 20 minutes, turn again and cook for a final 20 minutes or until the lamb is cooked to your liking.

Remove the lamb from the baking dish, cover and set aside. Skim the fat from the surface of the pan juices and discard. Slice the lamb and spoon over some of the pan juices to serve. SERVES 6-8

sherry-roasted lamb

SIDES AND SALADS

Pair your favourites from the weeknight and weekend chapters with the vibrant vegetable or salad dishes you'll find here. They're so good, some of them might work their way into your lunch repertoire, too!

celery AND apple salad

avocado, green bean AND quinoa salad

moroccan cauliflower salad

celery AND apple salad

1 small celeriac, peeled and cut into matchsticks
3 stalks celery, thinly sliced
20g small celery leaves
1 Granny Smith apple, thinly sliced
mustard dressing
1 heaped tablespoon wholegrain mustard
1 heaped tablespoon apple cider vinegar
1 heaped tablespoon apple juice
2 generous tablespoons extra virgin olive oil
sea salt and cracked black pepper

To make the mustard dressing, place the mustard, vinegar, juice, oil, salt and pepper in a bowl and whisk to combine. Arrange the the celeriac, celery, leaves and apple on plates and spoon over the dressing. SERVES 4

avocado, green bean AND quinoa salad

300g white quinoa
625ml water
2 generous tablespoons extra virgin olive oil
300g green beans, trimmed and blanched
1 avocado, cut into wedges
20g micro herbs* or small flat-leaf parsley leaves
preserved lemon dressing
2 generous tablespoons lemon juice
60ml extra virgin olive oil
2 teaspoons finely chopped preserved lemon rind*
2 teaspoons honey
1 heaped tablespoon finely chopped dill
sea salt and cracked black pepper

To make the preserved lemon dressing, place the lemon juice, oil, preserved lemon, honey, dill, salt and pepper in a bowl and whisk to combine. Set aside.
   Place the quinoa and water in a saucepan and allow to soak for 15 minutes. Place over high heat and bring to the boil. Reduce the heat to low, cover and cook for 15 minutes or until the water has been absorbed. Set aside to cool.
   Heat a large non-stick frying pan over high heat. Add the oil and quinoa and cook, stirring, for 8–10 minutes or until quinoa is light golden and crisp. Divide the quinoa between bowls with the beans, avocado and herbs and serve with the dressing. SERVES 4

moroccan cauliflower salad

1 x 1kg head cauliflower, trimmed and cut into thick slices
2 generous tablespoons extra virgin olive oil
5g small dill sprigs
sea salt and cracked black pepper
150g wild rocket leaves
20g flat-leaf parsley leaves
85g pomegranate seeds
tahini dressing
140g plain yoghurt
2 heaped tablespoons tahini paste*
2 generous tablespoons lemon juice
¼ teaspoon sea salt flakes
80ml water

Preheat oven to 180°C (350°F). To make the tahini dressing, combine the yoghurt, tahini, lemon juice, salt and water and whisk until smooth. Set aside.
   Combine the cauliflower, oil, dill, salt and pepper and toss to combine. Place on a large baking tray lined with non-stick baking paper and roast for 20–25 minutes or until the cauliflower is golden. Arrange the cauliflower, rocket and parsley on a serving platter and sprinkle with the pomegranate seeds. Serve with the tahini dressing. SERVES 4

This vibrant cauliflower salad is best served with any of the roasted lamb dishes.

rustic tomato salad <u>with</u> whipped feta

pickled carrot <u>and</u> radish salad

rustic tomato salad WITH whipped feta

600g mixed cherry tomatoes
1 heaped tablespoon finely chopped preserved lemon rind*
½ clove garlic, crushed
2 generous tablespoons lemon juice
2 teaspoons caster sugar
1 generous tablespoon extra virgin olive oil, plus extra,
    for drizzling
4 large slices sourdough bread, toasted
15g mint, shredded
15g baby basil leaves
sea salt and cracked black pepper
whipped feta
175g feta
125ml single cream*
2 teaspoons finely grated lemon zest
1 generous tablespoon lemon juice, extra

Cut a slit in the side of each tomato and squeeze to release the
juice and seeds. Place the tomatoes, preserved lemon, garlic,
lemon juice, sugar and oil in a glass or ceramic bowl and toss
to combine. Cover and refrigerate for 20 minutes to marinate.

To make the whipped feta, place the feta in a small food
processor and process until smooth. Add the cream, lemon zest
and juice and process until thick and just combined. Set aside.

Add the mint, basil, salt and pepper to the tomatoes and stir
to combine. Divide the sourdough between plates and spoon over
the tomato mixture. Serve with the whipped feta and drizzle with
extra oil. SERVES 4

pickled carrot AND radish salad

310ml water
250ml apple cider vinegar
75g caster sugar
4 sprigs dill
½ teaspoon juniper berries*, lightly crushed
24 baby carrots, peeled and trimmed
8 radishes, scrubbed, trimmed and thinly sliced
120g rocket leaves
300g labne* (yoghurt cheese)
1 heaped tablespoon za'atar*

Place the water, vinegar and sugar in a saucepan over high heat.
Stir until the sugar has dissolved. Boil for 2 minutes, remove from
the heat, add the dill and juniper and refrigerate until cold.

Blanch the carrots in boiling water for 30 seconds and refresh
immediately under cold water. Add the carrots and radishes to
the pickling liquid and pickle for 30 minutes.

Remove the vegetables from the pickling liquid and divide
between plates with the rocket and labne. Sprinkle the labne
with the za'atar to serve. SERVES 4

shoestring courgette fries

5 medium (600g) courgettes
vegetable oil, for deep-frying
150g plain flour
75g cornflour
1 teaspoon sea salt flakes
250ml milk
sea salt and lemon wedges, to serve

Trim the courgettes and slice into long, thin batons, discarding
the soft section in the middle with the seeds. Heat the oil in a
medium saucepan over high heat until the temperature reaches
180°C (350°F) on a kitchen thermometer. Combine the flour,
cornflour and salt. Dip a few courgette pieces at a time into the
milk and toss in the flour mixture, shaking off any excess.
Deep-fry the courgettes, in batches, for 3–5 minutes or until
golden. Drain on absorbent paper, sprinkle with the salt and serve
immediately with the lemon wedges. SERVES 4

shoestring courgette fries

spice-roasted carrot salad

golden baked onions

spice-roasted carrot salad

2 teaspoons ground cumin
60ml extra virgin olive oil
90g honey
60ml lemon juice
sea salt and cracked black pepper
6 carrots, peeled and quartered lengthways
2 teaspoons fennel seeds, lightly crushed
2 generous tablespoons pomegranate molasses*
150g rocket leaves
5g mint leaves
250g labne* (yoghurt cheese)

Preheat oven to 180°C (350°F). Place the cumin, oil, honey, lemon, salt and pepper in a large bowl and mix to combine. Place the carrots on a baking tray lined with non-stick baking paper, add the fennel seeds and toss to combine. Pour over half the honey mixture and toss to coat. Roast for 30 minutes or until soft and golden.

Divide the rocket and mint between plates and drizzle with the remaining honey dressing. Top with the carrots and spoon over the pomegranate molasses. Serve with the labne. SERVES 4

golden baked onions

6 onions, peeled and halved
1 generous tablespoon extra virgin olive oil
sea salt and cracked black pepper
250ml single cream*
1 heaped tablespoon thyme leaves
1 heaped tablespoon Dijon mustard
50g smoked mozzarella*, finely grated
60g Gruyère*, finely grated

Preheat oven to 180°C (350°F). Place the onions, cut-side up, in a greased baking dish. Drizzle with the oil and sprinkle with salt and pepper. Cover with aluminium foil and bake for 1½ hours. Uncover and bake for a further 15 minutes or until just starting to brown. Combine the cream, thyme, mustard and cheeses and spoon over the onions. Bake for a further 15–20 minutes or until the onions are golden. SERVES 6

whole herb-roasted cauliflower

3 litres chicken stock
8 sprigs sage
8 sprigs thyme
8 sprigs oregano
6 cloves garlic, skin on
1 x 600g head cauliflower
50g butter, melted
2 generous tablespoons extra virgin olive oil
sumac salt
1 teaspoon sea salt flakes
1 teaspoon sumac*
½ teaspoon dried chilli flakes

Preheat oven to 200°C (400°F). To make the sumac salt, combine the salt, sumac and chilli flakes and set aside.

Place the stock, sage, thyme, oregano and garlic in a deep saucepan over high heat and bring to the boil. Add the cauliflower, reduce the heat to low, cover and simmer for 8–10 minutes or until tender. Remove the cauliflower from the saucepan and strain the stock. Reserve the herbs and garlic and transfer to a baking tray lined with non-stick baking paper. Top with the cauliflower, spoon over the combined butter and oil and bake for 30–35 minutes or until golden. Serve the cauliflower with the sumac salt. SERVES 4–6

whole herb-roasted cauliflower

popovers

popovers

3 teaspoons vegetable oil
2 eggs, at room temperature
250ml milk, at room temperature
150g plain flour
½ teaspoon sea salt flakes
30g melted butter

Preheat oven to 220°C (425°F). Pour ½ teaspoon of vegetable oil into each hole of a 6-hole popover pan or muffin tin and place in the oven to heat. Place the eggs, milk, flour and salt in a blender and process to combine. Add the butter and process to just combine.

Remove the tray from the oven and pour 80ml of the mixture into each hole. Bake for 7 minutes, reduce the heat to 120°C (325°F) and bake for a further 10–15 minutes or until golden and dry to the touch. MAKES 6

RE-STYLE

FOR BREAKFAST *with bacon*
Stir 80g chopped, cooked bacon and 1 tablespoon thyme leaves through the batter before baking.

AS A SNACK *caramelised onion*
Stir 2 heaped tablespoons store-bought caramelised onion relish through the batter before baking.

fig, feta <u>and</u> rocket panzanella

baked lemon, parmesan AND basil risotto

miso-roasted aubergine

fig, feta AND rocket panzanella

6 figs, halved
250g torn sourdough bread
8 sprigs marjoram
250g feta, cut into 4 pieces
120g rocket leaves
honey dressing
2 generous tablespoons extra virgin olive oil
60ml red wine vinegar
90g honey
sea salt and cracked black pepper

Preheat oven to 220°C (425°F). To make the dressing, combine the oil, vinegar, honey, salt and pepper. Place the figs, sourdough and marjoram on a baking tray lined with non-stick baking paper. Pour over half the dressing and bake for 10–15 minutes or until golden. Divide the fig and bread mixture between plates with the feta and rocket. Spoon over the remaining dressing to serve. **SERVES 4**

baked lemon, parmesan AND basil risotto

30g butter
1 onion, finely chopped
2 heaped tablespoons lemon thyme leaves
2 cloves garlic, crushed
250g arborio rice
1 litre chicken stock
1 heaped tablespoon finely grated lemon zest
1 generous tablespoon lemon juice
80g Parmesan, finely grated, plus extra, to serve
sea salt and cracked black pepper
25g small basil leaves

Preheat oven to 200°C (400°F). Heat a heavy-based ovenproof saucepan over medium heat. Add the butter, onion and lemon thyme and cook for 5 minutes or until soft. Add the garlic and cook for 30 seconds. Add the rice and stock and cover with a tight-fitting lid. Transfer to the oven and bake for 30 minutes. Add the lemon zest and juice, Parmesan, salt and pepper and stir until the risotto is creamy. Sprinkle with the basil leaves and extra Parmesan to serve. **SERVES 4**

miso-roasted aubergine

4 small aubergines, halved
sea salt
55g white miso paste*
60ml mirin*
1 heaped tablespoon brown sugar
sesame seeds, for sprinkling
coriander leaves and sliced spring onions, to serve

Preheat oven to 200°C (400°F). Cut deep slits into the flesh of the aubergine. Sprinkle with salt and allow to stand for 20 minutes. Brush away the salt and any excess liquid with absorbent paper. Transfer, cut-side up, to a baking tray and roast for 30 minutes. Combine the miso, mirin and sugar and spoon over the aubergine. Sprinkle with the sesame seeds and roast for a further 15–20 minutes or until the aubergine is soft and well browned. Top with the coriander and spring onion to serve. **SERVES 4**

rustic vegetable pancetta gratin

baked semolina

rustic vegetable pancetta gratin

1 generous tablespoon extra virgin olive oil
180g diced pancetta*
1 onion, sliced
2 cloves garlic, crushed
1 heaped tablespoon lemon thyme leaves
2 courgettes, sliced
150g green beans, trimmed and halved lengthways
3 stems kale, stalks removed and roughly chopped
180g frozen peas
15g roughly chopped mint
200g feta, roughly chopped
125ml single cream*
sea salt and cracked black pepper
topping
210g chunky sourdough breadcrumbs
60g Parmesan, finely grated
1 heaped tablespoon rosemary leaves
2 generous tablespoons extra virgin olive oil

Preheat oven to 200°C (400°F). Heat a large ovenproof frying pan over high heat. Add the oil and pancetta and cook for 2 minutes. Add the onion, garlic and thyme and cook for 2–3 minutes or until golden. Add the courgettes, beans and kale and cook for 5 minutes or until soft. Add the peas, mint, feta, cream, salt and pepper and mix to combine. Remove from the heat and set aside.

To make the topping, combine the breadcrumbs, parmesan and rosemary. Cover the vegetables with the topping, drizzle with oil and bake for 12–14 minutes or until the topping is golden. SERVES 4

baked semolina

1.5 litres milk
60g butter
½ teaspoon sea salt flakes
240g semolina*
500ml single cream*
100g mozzarella, grated
60g Parmesan, grated

Place the milk, butter and salt in a saucepan over medium heat. Bring to the boil and add the semolina in a thin, steady stream, whisking continuously. Reduce the heat to medium-low and stir for 2–3 minutes or until the semolina is creamy and soft. Pour into a greased 20cm x 30cm rectangular tin and refrigerate for 2 hours or until firm.

Preheat oven to 180°C (350°F). Cut the semolina into 12 squares and place in a greased 3.5-litre-capacity baking dish. Pour over the cream and sprinkle with the cheeses. Bake for 30–40 minutes or until golden. SERVES 8

mozzarella salad WITH crispy brussels sprouts

2 x 125g buffalo mozzarellas, thickly sliced
3 green or red tomatoes, chopped
1 heaped tablespoon small oregano leaves
15g mint leaves, shredded
2 heaped tablespoons finely chopped white onion
2 generous tablespoons white balsamic vinegar*
2 generous tablespoons extra virgin olive oil
1 teaspoon caster sugar
sea salt and cracked black pepper
small mint leaves, extra, to serve
crispy brussels sprouts
400g Brussels sprouts, trimmed
3 generous tablespoons extra virgin olive oil
sea salt

Preheat oven to 180°C (350°F). To make the crispy Brussels sprouts, trim the stalk of the sprouts with a paring knife and separate the leaves. Place in a bowl with the oil and salt and toss to combine. Divide between 2 baking trays lined with non-stick baking paper and bake for 10–15 minutes or until golden and crisp.

Divide the mozzarella between plates. Combine the tomatoes, oregano, mint, onion, vinegar, oil, sugar, salt and pepper and spoon over the mozzarella. Top with the crispy Brussels sprouts and extra mint leaves to serve. SERVES 4

mozzarella salad <u>with</u> crispy brussels sprouts

BAKING

I love baking, but I'm often short on time.
That's why I've developed these easy recipes, with a
dough or batter you can whip in a food processor,
or a cake you can simply melt-and-mix in one bowl.

raisin, oat AND choc-chip cookies

chocolate chunk share cookie

orange AND almond cake

raisin, oat AND choc-chip cookies

120g brown sugar
75g caster sugar
1 teaspoon vanilla extract
175g unsalted butter, chopped
1 egg
150g plain flour
1 teaspoon bicarbonate of soda
180g rolled oats
105g raisins
150g dark chocolate, chopped

Preheat oven to 160°C (325°F). Place both the sugars, vanilla, butter and egg in the bowl of a food processor and process until well combined. Add the flour, bicarbonate of soda and oats and process until combined. Add the raisins and chocolate and using a spoon, mix to combine. Roll 1 tablespoon of dough at a time into balls and place on baking trays lined with non-stick baking paper, leaving room to spread. Bake for 10–12 minutes or until golden. Cool on the trays for 5 minutes before transferring to wire racks to cool completely. MAKES 24

chocolate chunk share cookie

85g unsalted butter, softened
135g brown sugar
55g caster sugar
1 egg
2 teaspoons vanilla extract
150g plain flour
⅛ teaspoon bicarbonate of soda
25g cocoa powder
50g milk chocolate, chopped
50g white chocolate, chopped
vanilla ice-cream and store-bought caramel sauce or
  dulce de leche*, to serve

Preheat oven to 160°C (325°F). Place the butter, both the sugars, egg, vanilla, flour, bicarbonate of soda and cocoa in a food processor and process until a dough forms. Press the dough out to a 26cm round on a baking tray lined with non-stick baking paper, scatter with the chocolate and lightly press the pieces into the dough. Bake for 15–20 minutes or until firm to the touch. Allow to cool slightly on the tray. Serve warm with ice-cream and caramel sauce. SERVES 6–8

orange AND almond cake

200g unsalted butter, softened
275g caster sugar
2 heaped tablespoons finely grated orange zest
360g ground almonds
5 eggs
150g plain flour
plain yoghurt, to serve
orange syrup
375ml orange juice
150g caster sugar
1 vanilla pod, split and seeds scraped

Preheat oven to 160°C (325°F). Place the butter and sugar in a food processor and process until well combined. Add the orange zest, almonds, eggs and flour and process until combined. Pour the mixture into a lightly greased 24cm round springform cake tin lined with non-stick baking paper. Bake for 1 hour or until cooked when tested with a skewer.

While the cake is baking, make the orange syrup. Place the orange juice, sugar, vanilla pod and seeds in a small saucepan over low heat and stir to dissolve the sugar. Bring to a simmer and cook for 10 minutes or until the mixture has thickened and is syrupy. Discard the vanilla pod and pour half the hot syrup over the hot cake. Stand in the tin for 10 minutes. Remove the cake from the tin and serve with the yoghurt and remaining syrup. SERVES 10–12

Want to know a little secret to making these simple treats fast? Throw the ingredients in a food processor – too easy.

chocolate pound cake

chocolate pound cake

100g cocoa powder, sifted
180ml boiling water
250g unsalted butter, softened
220g caster sugar
20g brown sugar
2 teaspoons vanilla extract
5 eggs
150g plain flour
chocolate glaze
100g dark chocolate
1 teaspoon vanilla extract
60ml single cream*

Preheat oven to 160°C (325°F). Place the cocoa and boiling water in a bowl and mix until smooth. Set aside.

Place the butter and both the sugars in the bowl of an electric mixer and beat on high speed for 6 minutes or until light and creamy. Add the vanilla, eggs and cocoa mixture and beat until well combined. Add the flour and mix until just combined. Pour the mixture into a lightly greased 21cm x 10cm loaf tin lined with non-stick baking paper. Bake for 1 hour 10 minutes or until cooked when tested with a skewer. Cool in the tin for 5 minutes before turning out on to a wire rack to cool completely.

To make the chocolate glaze, place the chocolate, vanilla and cream in a small saucepan over low heat and stir until smooth. Cool slightly before spreading over the cooled cake to serve.

SERVES 12

RE-STYLE

AFTER DINNER *mini desserts*

To make little cakes, bake the mixture in 12 x 125ml-capacity greased muffin tins for 25–28 minutes or until cooked when tested with a skewer. Cool and spoon over the chocolate glaze to serve. **MAKES 12**

SPECIAL OCCASION *layer cake*

To make a layer cake, slice the cake into 3 even layers. Whisk together 300ml double cream* with 1 heaped tablespoon sifted icing sugar and ½ teaspoon vanilla bean paste*. Spread the cream between the layers and spoon over the chocolate glaze to serve.

raspberry sponge cake slice

no-fail muffins

raspberry sponge cake slice

2 eggs
375ml whipping cream*
2 teaspoons vanilla extract
330g caster sugar
300g self-raising flour, sifted
fresh raspberries, to serve
vanilla cream
375ml whipping cream*
1 heaped tablespoon icing sugar, sifted
½ teaspoon vanilla bean paste*

Preheat oven to 170°C (350°F). Place the eggs, cream, vanilla and sugar in a bowl and whisk until well combined. Add the flour and whisk until just combined. Pour into a 20cm x 30cm rectangular tin lined with non-stick baking paper and even the top of the mixture with a palette knife. Bake for 40–45 minutes or until just firm to the touch. Cool in the tin for 5 minutes before transferring to a wire rack to cool completely.

To make the vanilla cream, whisk together the cream, sugar and vanilla until soft peaks form. Spread the cream over the sponge and serve with the raspberries. SERVES 12

no-fail muffins

375g self-raising flour
1 teaspoon baking powder
220g caster sugar
1 egg
125ml vegetable oil
2 teaspoons vanilla extract
180ml milk
450g frozen raspberries or blueberries
95g milk, dark or white chocolate chips

Preheat oven to 180°C (350°F). Place the flour, baking powder and sugar in a bowl and mix to combine. Place the egg, oil, vanilla and milk in a separate bowl and whisk until combined. Pour the egg mixture over the dry ingredients and mix until just combined. Add the berries and chocolate chips and mix until just combined. Spoon the mixture into 12 x 125ml-capacity muffin tins lined with paper cases. Bake for 25–30 minutes or until just cooked when tested with a skewer. MAKES 12

easiest banana bread

4 medium ripe bananas
125ml light-flavoured extra virgin olive oil
3 eggs
265g brown sugar
1 teaspoon vanilla extract
225g self-raising flour
1 teaspoon ground cinnamon

Preheat oven to 180°C (350°F). Place the bananas in a bowl and mash with a fork. Add the oil, eggs, sugar and vanilla and mix to combine. Add the flour and cinnamon and mix until combined. Pour into a 21cm x 10cm loaf tin lined with non-stick baking paper. Bake for 1 hour 10 minutes or until cooked when tested with a skewer. Allow to stand in the tin for 5 minutes before turning out onto a wire rack to cool completely. SERVES 10

A perfect snack or lunchbox treat, this one-bowl banana bread requires little effort for super tasty results.

easiest banana bread

food processor carrot cake

food processor carrot cake

400g carrots, peeled and roughly chopped
120g pecans
175g brown sugar
110g caster sugar
225g plain flour
1 teaspoon baking powder
1 teaspoon bicarbonate of soda
2 teaspoons ground cinnamon
125ml vegetable oil
70g plain yoghurt
2 eggs
2 teaspoons vanilla extract
cream cheese frosting
250g cream cheese, softened
50g fresh ricotta

55g icing sugar
1 generous tablespoon lemon juice
1 teaspoon vanilla bean paste*

Preheat oven to 160°C (325°F). Place the carrot and pecans in a food processor and process until finely chopped. Add both the sugars, flour, baking powder, bicarbonate of soda, cinnamon, oil, yoghurt, eggs and vanilla, and pulse in short bursts until combined. Pour the mixture into a 22cm round springform cake tin lined with non-stick baking paper and bake for 55–60 minutes or until just cooked when tested with a skewer. Cool in the tin.

To make the cream cheese frosting, place the cream cheese, ricotta, sugar, lemon and vanilla in a food processor and process until smooth. Spread the frosting over the cooled cake to serve.
SERVES 10–12

RE-STYLE

AFTERNOON TEA *chic cupcakes*
To make cupcakes, follow the above recipe using ½ teaspoon of the bicarbonate of soda. Spoon the mixture into 20 x 125ml-capacity muffin tins lined with cupcake cases and bake for 25–30 minutes or until cooked when tested with a skewer. Pipe or spread with frosting to serve.

SUMMER PICNIC *add mango*
To make a layer cake, halve the cake and fill with the frosting. Top with 2 peeled and sliced mangoes and sandwich with the top of the cake. Dust with icing sugar to finish.

peanut butter AND chocolate fondants

salted caramel chocolate brownie

salted caramel chocolate brownie

120g plain flour
⅛ teaspoon baking powder
220g brown sugar
2 eggs
120g store-bought caramel filling or dulce de leche*
2 teaspoons vanilla extract
150g unsalted butter, melted
150g dark chocolate, chopped
½ teaspoon sea salt flakes

Preheat oven to 160°C (325°F). Place the flour, baking powder and sugar in a bowl and mix to combine. Add the eggs, caramel, vanilla and butter and whisk until smooth. Stir though the chocolate and spoon the mixture into a 20cm square cake tin lined with non-stick baking paper. Sprinkle with the sea salt and bake for 40–45 minutes or until just firm around the edges. Cut into squares and serve warm or cold. MAKES 16 SQUARES

preserved lemon yoghurt cake

150g unsalted butter, softened
220g caster sugar
2 heaped tablespoons finely chopped preserved lemon rind*
1 teaspoon vanilla extract
3 eggs
280g plain yoghurt
300g self-raising flour, sifted
lemon icing
320g icing sugar, sifted
2 teaspoons lemon juice
2 heaped tablespoons plain yoghurt

Preheat oven to 160°C (325°F). Place the butter, sugar, lemon rind and vanilla in the bowl of a food processor and process until the mixture is pale and creamy. Add the eggs and yoghurt and process to combine. Add the flour and process until the mixture is just combined. Spoon into a 24cm lightly greased fluted ring or Bundt tin. Bake for 40–45 minutes or until cooked when tested with a skewer. Cool in the tin for 5 minutes before inverting onto a wire rack to cool completely.

To make the lemon icing, place the icing sugar, lemon juice and yoghurt in a bowl and mix until smooth. Spoon over the cooled cake to serve. SERVES 10

peanut butter AND chocolate fondants

140g crunchy peanut butter
50g unsalted butter, softened
110g caster sugar
45g brown sugar
1 egg
100g plain flour, sifted
½ teaspoon baking powder, sifted
8 squares dark chocolate
double cream* or vanilla ice-cream, to serve

Preheat oven to 160°C (325°F). Place the peanut butter, butter, both the sugars and egg in the bowl of an electric mixer and beat until pale and creamy. Stir though the flour and baking powder. Divide half the mixture between 4 x 180ml-capacity greased dariole moulds. Place 2 squares of chocolate, upright and back-to-back, into each fondant and spoon over the remaining mixture so it comes three-quarters up the sides of the moulds. Bake for 20–25 minutes or until just firm. Stand for 5 minutes before inverting onto plates. Serve warm with double cream or vanilla ice-cream. SERVES 4

preserved lemon yoghurt cake

cheat's lemon meringue tarts

cheat's lemon meringue tarts

8 thin plain sweet biscuits
350g store-bought lemon curd*
meringue topping
165g caster sugar
60ml water
2 egg whites

To make the meringue topping, place the sugar and water in a saucepan over medium-low heat and stir until the sugar is dissolved. Simmer for 3 minutes and remove from the heat.

Using a hand-held electric mixer, beat the egg whites until soft peaks form. Add the sugar syrup in a thin, steady stream and beat until the meringue is thick and glossy. Top each biscuit with a little lemon curd and spoon over some of the meringue. Slightly brown the meringue with a small kitchen blowtorch until the edges are golden to serve. **MAKES 12**

RE-STYLE

FLAVOUR VARIATION *passionfruit*
Use 350g passionfruit curd instead of lemon curd.

MAKE IT PORTABLE *picnic treat*
Place the biscuits into the bases of thick glass jars. Top with the curd and meringue. Use caution when blow-torching the tops.

cheat's scrunched baklava

simple baked passionfruit cheesecakes

cheat's scrunched baklava

105g pistachios
105g walnuts
120g almonds
2 teaspoons ground cinnamon
110g caster sugar
10 sheets filo pastry*
200g unsalted butter, melted
slivered or chopped pistachios, to serve
sugar syrup
220g caster sugar
125ml water
1 heaped tablespoon shredded orange zest

Preheat oven to 180°C (350°F). Place the pistachios, walnuts, almonds, cinnamon and sugar in a food processor and pulse until finely chopped. Brush 1 sheet of filo pastry with butter and cut in half. Sprinkle half the sheet with the nut mixture and fold over the pastry to enclose. Scrunch the pastry into a ball, folding any of the loose pastry ends underneath. Place in a lightly greased 20cm x 30cm rectangular tin. Repeat with remaining pastry sheets. Bake for 15–20 minutes or until a deep golden colour.

While the baklava is baking, make the sugar syrup. Place the sugar, water and orange zest in a saucepan over medium heat. Stir gently until the sugar has dissolved. Bring the syrup to the boil and simmer for 5 minutes or until thickened.

Pour three-quarters of the hot syrup over the cooked baklava and stand for 5 minutes before serving. Sprinkle with the pistachios and serve with the remaining syrup. **SERVES 16**

No need to layer and butter sheets of filo pastry for this very simple cheat's baklava. Just scrunch and bake.

simple baked passionfruit cheesecakes

165g cream cheese, chopped
250g fresh ricotta
2 eggs
165g caster sugar
2 generous tablespoons lemon juice
1 level tablespoon cornflour
1 generous tablespoon water
60ml fresh passionfruit pulp
12 plain sweet biscuits

Preheat oven to 150°C (300°F). Place the cream cheese, ricotta, eggs, sugar and lemon in the bowl of a food processor. Combine the cornflour and water and mix to a smooth paste. Add to the cream cheese mixture and process until smooth. Stir through the passionfruit.

Line 12 x 125ml-capacity muffin tins with paper cases. Place a biscuit into the base of each and pour over the cheesecake mixture. Bake for 20–25 minutes or until just set. Refrigerate until cold. **MAKES 12**

fig, goat's cheese AND honey tarts

200g store-bought sweet shortcrust pastry sheet*
100g soft goat's cheese
100g fresh ricotta
1 heaped tablespoon caster sugar
1 teaspoon finely grated lemon zest
4 fresh figs, sliced
2 generous tablespoons honey
1 tablespoon lemon thyme leaves

Preheat oven to 180°C (350°F). Cut the pastry into 4 x 12 cm rounds. Combine the goat's cheese, ricotta, sugar and lemon zest and mix until smooth. Spread the mixture over the pastry leaving a 1cm border. Bake for 15–20 minutes or until golden. Top with the figs, drizzle with honey and sprinkle with the thyme to serve. **SERVES 4**

Tip: see glossary to make your own sweet shortcrust pastry.

fig, goat's cheese AND honey tarts

melt AND mix vanilla cupcakes

melt AND mix vanilla cupcakes

250g plain flour
½ teaspoon baking powder
¼ teaspoon bicarbonate of soda
220g caster sugar
125g unsalted butter, melted and cooled slightly
1 egg
180ml milk
60g sour cream
2 teaspoons vanilla extract
white chocolate frosting
125ml whipping cream*
250g white chocolate, chopped
1 teaspoon vanilla bean paste*

Preheat oven to 160°C (325°F). Place the flour, baking powder, bicarbonate of soda and sugar in a bowl and mix to combine. Add the butter, egg, milk, sour cream and vanilla and whisk until just combined. Spoon into 12 x 125ml-capacity muffin tins lined with paper cases. Bake for 25–30 minutes or until cooked when tested with a skewer. Transfer to a wire rack to cool.

To make the white chocolate frosting, place the cream in a small saucepan over low heat and cook until the cream is hot but not boiling. Add the chocolate and stir until melted and smooth. Transfer to a bowl and place in the fridge until just cool. Add the vanilla and, using a hand-held electric mixer, whisk on medium speed until soft peaks form. Spread the frosting over the cooled cakes to serve. MAKES 12

RE-STYLE

GIRLS' PICNIC *butterfly cakes*
To make butterfly cupcakes, cut a small round from the top of each cake and cut in half. Fill the holes with jam and some of the frosting. Replace the tops as shown and dust with icing sugar to finish.

HIGH-TEA TREAT *curd and cream*
To make filled cupcakes, cut a small round from the top of each cake and reserve. Fill the holes with some of the frosting and a little lemon or passionfruit curd*. Replace the tops and dust with icing sugar to finish.

DESSERTS

No-one wants to miss out on dessert, so I've created these irresistable treats that are super easy to make, whether it's a cheat's take on a classic, a sweet you can make ahead, or something seasonal, simply prepared.

caramelised plums WITH chai granita

peach melba WITH coconut praline

peaches IN bellini syrup

caramelised plums WITH chai granita

6 plums, halved and stones removed
55g caster sugar
chai granita
3 chai (spiced) tea bags
110g caster sugar
250ml boiling water
750ml milk

To make the chai granita, place the tea bags, sugar and water in
a saucepan over medium heat and cook, stirring, for 2 minutes or
until the sugar has dissolved and the tea has infused. Remove from
the heat, discard the tea bags and add the milk. Pour the mixture
into a shallow metal container and allow to cool. Freeze for 4 hours
or until firm.

Place the plums, cut-side up, on a baking tray, sprinkle with
the sugar and cook under a preheated hot grill for 8–10 minutes
or until caramelised. Divide the plums between bowls. Scrape the
top of the granita with a fork and spoon over the plums to serve.
SERVES 4

peach melba WITH coconut praline

2 white peaches, halved and stones removed
220g caster sugar
500ml water
store-bought raspberry sorbet, to serve
coconut praline
110g caster sugar
15g flaked coconut*

Preheat oven to 200°C (400°F). To make the coconut praline,
sprinkle the sugar evenly over a baking tray lined with non-stick
baking paper. Bake for 8 minutes or until the sugar has turned
light golden. Sprinkle with the coconut and allow to stand for
10 minutes to set. Break into large pieces and set aside.

Place the peaches, sugar and water in a medium saucepan over
high heat and bring to the boil. Reduce the heat to low and simmer
for 4–5 minutes or until just tender. Remove with a slotted spoon
and gently peel the peaches, discarding the skins. Set aside.
Simmer the poaching syrup for a further 8–10 minutes or until
thickened slightly. Set aside to cool.

Divide the peaches between plates and top with a scoop of
raspberry sorbet. Spoon over some of the poaching syrup and
serve with the coconut praline. SERVES 4

peaches IN bellini syrup

750ml prosecco (sparkling wine)
220g caster sugar
1 vanilla pod, split and seeds scraped
2 pieces lemon peel
6 yellow peaches
vanilla ice-cream, to serve

Place the prosecco, sugar, vanilla pod and seeds and lemon
in a saucepan over high heat, bring to the boil and stir until the
sugar has dissolved. Reduce the heat to medium-low. Add the
peaches and simmer for 6–8 minutes or until the peaches are
soft. Remove with a slotted spoon and gently peel the peaches,
discarding the skin. Set aside for 5 minutes to cool. Return the
peaches to the syrup and refrigerate until cold.

Divide the peaches between bowls and pour over the syrup.
Serve with vanilla ice-cream. SERVES 6

*Sweet stonefruit needs little
work to let its flavours shine
in desserts. Keep it simple.*

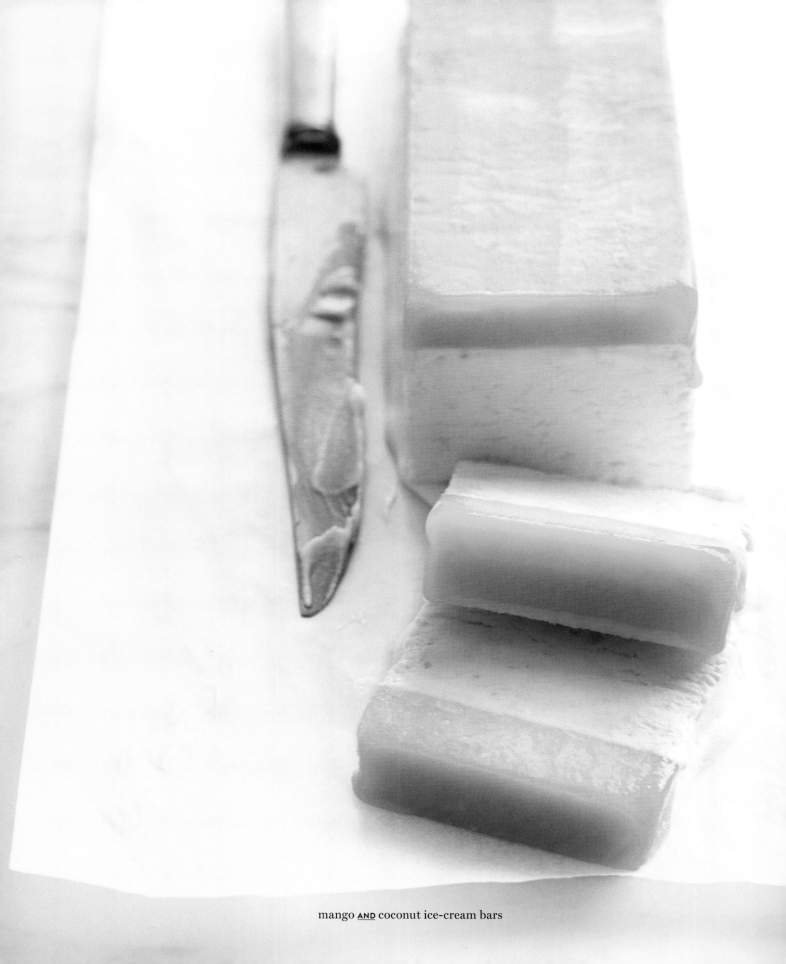

mango <u>AND</u> coconut ice-cream bars

mango AND coconut ice-cream bars

250ml mango purée
55g caster sugar
coconut semifreddo
2 eggs
2 egg yolks, extra
165g caster sugar
250ml whipping cream*
60ml coconut cream*, chilled
20g desiccated coconut*, toasted

Combine the mango purée and sugar and stir until the sugar is dissolved. Pour into the base of a 32cm x 8cm loaf tin lined with non-stick baking paper and freeze until set.

To make the coconut semifreddo, place the eggs, extra yolks and sugar in a heatproof bowl over a saucepan of simmering water. Using a hand-held electric mixer, whisk for 6–8 minutes or until pale and thick. Remove from the heat and whisk for a further 2 minutes. Set aside. Pour the cream and coconut cream into a separate bowl and whisk until soft peaks form. Fold the egg mixture through the cream with the desiccated coconut and pour into the tin over the mango layer. Freeze for 4 hours or until set. Remove the bar from the tin and slice to serve. SERVES 8–10

RE-STYLE

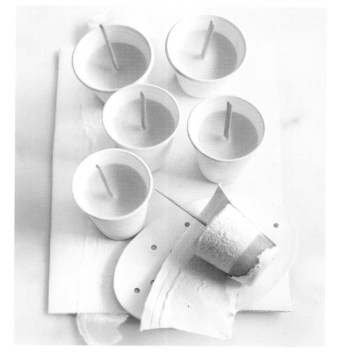

CHIC DINNER *single serve*
To make individual frozen desserts, simply layer the mixture between 8 x 375ml-capacity glasses following the above method.

GARDEN PARTY *simple lollies*
To make ice lollies, divide the mixture between 8 x 375ml-capacity paper cups. Insert ice lolly sticks once the mango layer has frozen.

caramel banana puddings

caramelised banana split

caramel banana puddings

60g unsalted butter, softened
60g brown sugar
2 heaped tablespoons caster sugar
1 medium banana, mashed
1 egg
100g self-raising flour
double cream* or ice-cream, to serve
caramel sauce
135g brown sugar
80ml boiling water
180ml single cream*

Preheat oven to 190°C (375°F). Place the butter, both the sugars, banana, egg and flour in a food processor and process until smooth. Spoon the mixture into 4 x 180ml-capacity lightly greased ovenproof ramekins.

To make the caramel sauce, place the sugar and water in a jug and stir until the sugar is dissolved. Add the cream and stir to combine. Pour the sauce over the puddings and bake for 20–25 minutes or until golden. MAKES 4

caramelised banana split

4 medium bananas, peeled and halved lengthways
110g caster sugar
vanilla ice-cream and store-bought caramel sauce, to serve
candied almonds
80g flaked almonds
80g icing sugar
2 generous tablespoons water

Preheat oven to 180°C (350°F). To make the candied almonds, place the almonds, sugar and water in a bowl and toss to coat. Transfer to a baking tray lined with non-stick baking paper and bake for 12–14 minutes or until golden. Allow to cool, break into pieces and set aside.

Place the bananas on a metal tray and sprinkle with the caster sugar. Using a small kitchen blowtorch, or a hot grill, caramelise the tops of the bananas until golden. Divide the bananas between plates and top with scoops of vanilla ice-cream.

Drizzle with the caramel sauce and sprinkle with the candied almonds to serve. SERVES 4

coconut AND passionfruit cream pie

150g plain sweet biscuits, crushed
25g desiccated coconut*, toasted
100g unsalted butter, melted
coconut filling
375ml double or whipping cream*
180ml coconut cream*
3 heaped tablespoons icing sugar
350g store-bought passionfruit curd*
fresh passionfruit pulp, to serve

Place the biscuits, coconut and butter in a bowl and mix to combine. Using the back of metal spoon, press the mixture into the base and sides of a shallow 24cm pie tin and refrigerate until firm.

To make the coconut filling, place the cream, coconut cream and sugar in a bowl and whisk until thickened. Spread the passionfruit curd over the base of the pie, spoon over the cream filling and refrigerate for 30 minutes or until set. Cut the pie into wedges and top with passionfruit pulp to serve. SERVES 8

This no-bake pie is simple to prepare using only a few store-bought ingredients.

coconut AND passionfruit cream pie

nectarine AND coconut tart

nectarine **AND** coconut tart

200g store-bought sweet shortcrust pastry sheet*
75g shredded or dessicated coconut
1 egg white
55g caster sugar
2 nectarines, thinly sliced
caster sugar, extra, for sprinkling
double cream*, to serve

Preheat oven to 180°C (350°F). Cut the pastry into a 24cm round and place on a baking tray lined with non-stick baking paper. Mix to combine the coconut, egg white and sugar and spread over the pastry, leaving a 1cm border. Top with the nectarine slices and fold over the edges of the pastry to form a border. Sprinkle with the extra sugar and bake for 16–20 minutes or until golden. Cut into wedges and serve hot or cold with double cream.

Tip: see glossary to make your own sweet shortcrust pastry.

RE-STYLE

SATURDAY PICNIC *cut into squares*
Cut the pastry sheet in half to make two 24cm x 12cm rectangles. Top with the coconut mixture and the nectarines leaving a 1cm border. Bake for 20–25 minutes or until golden. Combine lemon zest and sugar and sprinkle over the tart to serve.

SUNDAY LUNCH *small and elegant*
Cut 4 x 10cm rounds from the pastry and top with the coconut mixture and nectarines. Bake for 15–18 minutes or until golden. Serve with double cream or vanilla ice-cream.

strawberries <u>WITH</u> balsamic toffee

summer fruits <u>with</u> mint sugar

strawberries WITH balsamic toffee

350g strawberries, hulled and sliced
2 teaspoons vanilla bean paste*
2 heaped tablespoons icing sugar
1 teaspoon water
15g small basil leaves
420g plain sheep's milk yoghurt
balsamic toffee
220g caster sugar
2 generous tablespoons balsamic vinegar

Preheat oven 200°C (400°F). To make the balsamic toffee, place the sugar and balsamic in a bowl and mix to combine. Spread evenly onto 2 baking trays lined with non-stick baking paper and bake for 8 minutes or until bubbling and caramelised. Set aside to cool and harden, roughly chop and set aside.

Place the strawberries, vanilla, sugar and water in a bowl and toss to combine. Divide the yoghurt between glasses and top with the strawberries, basil leaves and balsamic toffee to serve. SERVES 4

summer fruits WITH mint sugar

5g mint leaves
1 teaspoon finely grated lemon zest
½ vanilla pod, split and seeds scraped
110g caster sugar
2 peaches, halved, stones removed and sliced
2 nectarines, halved, stones removed and sliced
2 plums, halved, stones removed and sliced
1 mango, peeled and cut into wedges

Place the mint, lemon, vanilla seeds and sugar in a food processor and process until well combined.

Place the fruit in a large bowl and sprinkle with ¾ of the mint sugar. Allow to stand for 20 minutes to marinate. Divide the fruit between plates and sprinkle with the remaining mint sugar to serve. SERVES 4–6

pine-lime granita

220g caster sugar
375ml water
500ml pineapple juice
80ml lime juice
vanilla cream
180ml double or whipping cream*
1 heaped tablespoon icing sugar
½ teaspoon vanilla bean paste*

Place the water and sugar in a saucepan over low heat and stir to dissolve. Remove from the heat and refrigerate until cold. Add the pineapple and lime juice to the cooled syrup, pour into a shallow metal container and freeze for 4 hours or until firm. Rake the granita with a fork and return to the freezer.

To make the vanilla cream, place the cream, sugar and vanilla in a bowl and whisk until soft peaks form. Spoon the granita into bowls and top with the vanilla cream to serve. SERVES 4–6

Paired with creamy vanilla, this pine-lime granita evokes memories of summer holidays.

pine-lime granita

salted chocolate caramel tart

salted chocolate caramel tart

150g unsalted butter, softened
110g icing sugar
35g cocoa powder
225g plain flour
2 egg yolks
1 teaspoon vanilla extract
sea salt, to serve
caramel filling
180ml single cream*
90g unsalted butter
330g caster sugar
125ml water
½ teaspoon sea salt flakes
chocolate glaze
125ml single cream*
125g dark chocolate, chopped

Preheat oven to 180°C (350°F). Place the butter and sugar in a food processor and process until pale. Add the cocoa, flour, egg and vanilla and process to a smooth dough. Press into the base and sides of a 26cm loose-bottomed, fluted tart tin to 5mm thick. Trim the edges and refrigerate until firm. Prick the dough with a fork and bake for 15 minutes or until the pastry is cooked. Set aside. To make the filling, place the cream and butter in a saucepan over medium heat until melted. Set aside. Place the sugar and water in a saucepan over low heat and stir until the sugar has dissolved. Increase the heat to high and boil, without stirring, until dark golden and the mixture reaches 170°C (340°F) on a sugar thermometer. Remove from the heat and carefully whisk in the cream mixture. Return the pan to low heat and stir for 5 minutes or until thickened. Pour into the pastry shell and refrigerate until firm. To make the glaze, place the cream in a saucepan over low heat. Add the chocolate and stir until melted and smooth. Pour the chocolate over the caramel and refrigerate until firm. Sprinkle with salt and cut into wedges to serve. **SERVES 8–10**

RE-STYLE

FRIDAY DINNER *elegant slices*
Press the dough into a 35cm x 12cm loose-bottomed, fluted rectangular tart tin and cook as per the above recipe. (You will have leftover dough and caramel.)

SUNDAY LUNCH *mini serves*
Press the dough into 6 x 11cm loose-bottomed fluted tart tins and cook as per the above recipe.

chocolate dutch pancake

tiramisu ice-cream

raspberry pavlova ice-cream

chocolate dutch pancake

75g plain flour
2 heaped tablespoons cocoa powder
45g brown sugar
2 heaped tablespoons caster sugar
2 eggs
125ml milk
1 teaspoon vanilla extract
30g unsalted butter
vanilla ice-cream and fresh raspberries, to serve

Preheat oven to 190°C (375°F). Place a 20cm ovenproof frying pan in the oven to heat for 10 minutes. Place the flour, cocoa, both the sugars, eggs, milk and vanilla in a food processor and process until smooth.

Melt the butter in the hot frying pan and swirl to coat. Pour the batter into the pan and bake for 15–20 minutes or until the pancake is puffed and firm around the edges. Top with ice-cream and raspberries to serve. SERVES 4

Take a classic dessert like pavlova or tiramisu and turn it into a frozen delight.

tiramisu ice-cream

2 litres vanilla ice-cream
6 sponge finger biscuits
125ml coffee-flavoured liqueur
100g dark chocolate, grated

Place the ice-cream in the bowl of an electric mixer and beat for 2 minutes or until softened and smooth. Spoon half the ice cream into a metal container. Dip the biscuits into the liqueur and press into the tin. Sprinkle over half the grated chocolate and spoon over the remaining ice-cream. Sprinkle with the remaining chocolate and freeze until firm. SERVES 6

raspberry pavlova ice-cream

2 litres vanilla ice-cream
100g store-bought meringues, crumbled
160g raspberry jam

Place the ice-cream in the bowl of an electric mixer and beat for 2 minutes or until softened and smooth. Fold through the meringue and jam and spoon into a metal container. Freeze for 4 hours or until firm. SERVES 4-6

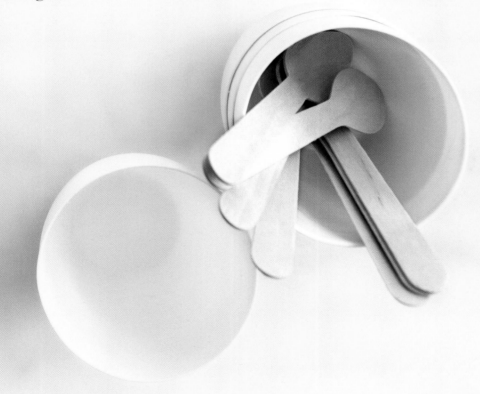

no-fail soufflé

no-fail soufflé

melted unsalted butter, for greasing
caster sugar, for dusting
150ml fresh passionfruit pulp
55g caster sugar
2 generous tablespoons lemon juice
1 heaped tablespoon cornflour
3 teaspoons water
4 egg whites
110g caster sugar, extra
vanilla ice-cream, to serve

Preheat oven to 170°C (325°F). Brush 4 x 375ml-capacity ovenproof ramekins with butter, dust well with sugar and place on a baking tray.

Place the passionfruit, sugar and lemon juice in a saucepan over medium heat and stir to dissolve the sugar. Combine the cornflour and water and whisk to a smooth paste. Whisk the cornflour mixture into the passionfruit mixture and stir for 1 minute or until thickened. Remove from the heat and spoon the mixture into a bowl. Refrigerate until cold.

Place the egg whites in a bowl and beat with a hand-held electric mixer until soft peaks form. Add the extra sugar in a thin, steady stream and beat until the mixture is thick and glossy. Fold the egg whites through the passionfruit mixture and spoon into the prepared ramekins. Bake for 10–12 minutes or until the soufflés have risen and feel just set to the touch. Serve immediately with ice-cream. **SERVES 4**

RE-STYLE

RIPPER RASPBERRY *tart and sweet*
To make raspberry-flavoured soufflés, replace the passionfruit with 150ml of blended and strained fresh raspberries.

LEMON DELICIOUS *fresh and tangy*
To make lemon-flavoured soufflés, replace the passionfruit with 150ml of lemon juice, dropping the 2 tablespoons of juice in the original recipe.

GLOSSARY AND INDEX

Ingredients marked with an asterisk are listed in the GLOSSARY, *as well as basic information on staple ingredients. There's also a useful list of global* MEASURES, *temperatures and common* CONVERSIONS. *To make recipes easier to find, they are listed alphabetically in the* INDEX *and also by main ingredient.*

BASICS

butter
Unless stated otherwise in a recipe, butter should be at room temperature for cooking. It should not be half-melted or too soft to handle, and we use unsalted butter in baked goods.

butter beans
Large, plump white beans also known as lima beans. They go well in soups, stews and salads. Available from delicatessens and supermarkets either tinned or in dried form. Dried beans need to be soaked in water before cooking.

capers
The small green flower buds of the caper bush. Available packed either in brine or salt. Before use, rinse thoroughly, drain and pat dry.

cheese

mozzarella
Italian in origin, mozzarella is the mild cheese of pizza, lasagne and tomato salads. It's made by cutting and spinning (or stringing) the curd to achieve a smooth, elastic consistency. The most prized variety is made from buffalo's milk.

Parmesan
Italy's favourite hard, granular cheese is made from cow's milk. Parmigiano reggiano is the best variety, made under strict guidelines in the Emilia-Romagna region and aged for an average of two years. Grana padano mainly comes from Lombardy and is aged for 15 months.

ricotta
A creamy, finely grained white cheese. Ricotta means 'recooked' in Italian, a reference to the way the cheese is produced by heating the whey left over from making other cheese varieties. It's fresh and creamy and low in fat.

chickpeas
A legume native to western Asia and across the Mediterranean, the chickpea is used in soups, stews and is the base ingredient in the Middle Eastern dip, hummus. Dried chickpeas must be soaked before cooking, but you can also buy them tinned.

chillies
There are over 200 different types of chilli in the world. By general rule of thumb, long red or green chillies are milder, fruitier and sweeter, while small chillies are much hotter. Remove the membranes and seeds for a milder result in a dish.

coriander
This pungent green herb is common in Asian and Mexican cooking. The finely chopped roots are sometimes incorporated in curry pastes. The dried seeds are an Indian staple, sold ground or whole, and one of the base ingredients in curry. The dried form can not be substituted for fresh.

couscous
The name given to both the national dish of Algeria, Tunisia and Morocco and the tiny grains of flour-coated semolina that make it. We use the instant variety in our recipes. For a better flavour, use stock rather than water to soak the couscous.

dijon mustard
Also known as French mustard, this is a pale, creamy and mildly flavoured mustard originating in France. It's commonly used in a vinaigrette.

eggs
The standard egg size used in this book is 60g. It is important to use the right size eggs for a recipe, as this will affect the outcome of baked goods. The correct volume is especially important when using egg whites to make meringues. You should use eggs at room temperature for baking.

flour
Made from ground cereal grains, flour is the primary ingredient in breads, cakes and many other baked goods including biscuits, pastries, pizzas and pie cases.

cornflour
When made from ground corn or maize, cornflour is a gluten-free flour. It is often blended with water or stock to use as a thickening agent. Not to be confused with cornflour in the United States, which is finely ground corn meal.

plain
Ground from the endosperm of wheat, plain white flour contains no raising agent.

rice
A fine flour made from ground white rice. Used as a thickening agent, in baking and to coat foods when cooking Asian dishes, particularly those needing a crispy finish, such as tofu or chicken.

self-raising
Ground from the endosperm of wheat, self-raising flour contains raising agents including sodium carbonates and calcium phosphates. To make it using plain flour, add 1½ teaspoons of baking powder for every 150g of flour.

ground almonds
Also known as almond meal, almonds are available from most supermarkets. Make your own by processing whole skinned almonds to a fine meal in a food processor or blender. To remove the skins from almonds, soak in boiling water, then, using your fingers, slip the skins off.

horseradish
A pungent root vegetable that releases mustard oil when cut or grated. Commonly sold as grated horseradish or horseradish cream. Used as a condiment, it is a superb partner for pork and roast beef. Available fresh from greengrocers or in jars from the supermarket and delicatessens.

lemongrass

A tall lemon-scented grass used in Asian cooking, particularly in Thai dishes. Peel away the outer leaves and chop the tender white root-end finely, or add in large pieces during cooking and remove before serving. If adding in large pieces, bruise them with the back of a large knife.

maple syrup

A sweetener made from the sap of the maple tree. Be sure to use pure maple syrup rather than imitation or pancake syrup, which is made from corn syrup flavoured with maple and does not have the same intensity of flavour.

noodles

Keep a supply of dried noodles in the pantry for last-minute meals. Fresh noodles will keep in the fridge for a week. Available from supermarkets and Asian food stores.

cellophane (bean thread)

Also called mung bean vermicelli or glass noodles, these noodles are very thin and almost transparent. Soak them in boiling water and drain well to prepare for use.

dried rice

Fine, dried noodles common in southeast Asian cooking. Depending on their thickness, rice noodles need only be boiled briefly, or soaked in hot water until soft.

rice vermicelli

Very thin dried rice noodles sometimes called rice sticks. They are usually used in soups such as laksa and in salads.

soba

Japanese noodles made from buckwheat and wheat flour, soba are greyish brown in colour and served in cold salads or in hot soups.

udon

This thick Japanese wheat noodle is commonly used in soups.

olives

black

Black olives are more mature and less salty than the green variety. Choose firm olives with good colour and a fruity taste.

green

Green olives are picked when unripe, which makes them denser in texture than black olives. The Sicilian variety of green olives are plump and fruity.

oil

Olive oil is graded according to its flavour, aroma and acidity. Extra virgin is the highest quality oil; it contains no more than 1 per cent acid. Virgin is the next best; it contains 1.5 per cent or less acid. Bottles labelled 'olive oil' contain a combination of refined and unrefined virgin olive oil. Light olive oil is the least pure in quality and intensity of flavour.

tapenade

Paste made by blending olives, capers, garlic and anchovies with oil. Served as a dip with crackers, or spread on bruschetta and pizzas, it makes a good marinade and partner for cold meats or cheeses.

pistachio

A delicately flavoured green nut inside a hard outer shell, pistachios are available salted or unsalted. They're used in Middle Eastern cuisine as well as in salads and sweets, such as baklava.

prosciutto

Italian ham that's been salted and dried for up to two years. The paper-thin slices are eaten raw or used to lend their distinctive flavour to braises and other cooked dishes.

polenta

Used extensively in northern Italy, this corn meal is cooked in simmering water until it has a porridge-like consistency. In this form it is enriched with butter and cheese to serve with meat dishes.

sesame seeds

These small seeds have a strong nutty flavour and can be used in savoury and sweet cooking. White sesame seeds are the most common variety, but black, or unhulled, seeds are popular for coatings in Asian cooking as well as some Asian desserts. Sesame oil is made by extracting the oil from roasted seeds.

star anise

A small brown seed-cluster that is shaped like a star. It has a strong aniseed flavour and can be used whole or ground in sweet and savoury dishes. It works well in master stocks or braises.

sugar

Extracted as crystals from the juice of the sugar cane plant or beet, sugar is a sweetener, flavour enhancer, bulking agent and preservative.

brown

Processed with molasses, it comes in differing shades of brown, according to the quantity of molasses added, which varies between countries. This also affects the taste of the sugar, and therefore the end product.

caster

Gives baked products a light texture and crumb, which is important for many cakes and light desserts such as meringues. It dissolves easily.

icing

Regular granulated sugar ground to a very fine powder. It often clumps together and needs to be sieved before using. Use pure icing sugar not icing sugar mixture, which contains cornflour and needs more liquid.

white

Regular granulated sugar is used in baking when a light texture is not crucial. The crystals are large, so you need to beat, add liquids or heat this sugar to dissolve it.

tarragon

Called the king of herbs by the French and used in many of their classic sauces such as Bérnaise and tartare. It has a slight aniseed flavour.

tomato

bottled tomato sauce
Sometimes labelled 'passata' or 'sugo'. Italian for 'passed', passata is made by removing the skins and seeds from ripe tomatoes and passing the flesh through a sieve to make a thick, rich, pulpy tomato purée. Sugo is made from crushed tomatoes, so it has a little more texture than passata. Both are available in bottles from supermarkets.

heirloom
A non-hybrid cultivar of tomato usually not grown on a commercial scale, heirlooms are large with a bumpy appearance and good, strong flavour. You can find heirloom tomatoes in rich reds, green and yellow.

passata
Puréed and seived tomatoes in a tin or jar. (not tomato purée). Substitute with fresh or tinned peeled and puréed tomatoes.

purée
This double-concentrated tomato purée is used as a flavour booster and thickener in soups, sauces and stews. There are also salt-reduced versions available.

vanilla pods

These fragrant cured pods from the vanilla orchid are used whole, often split with the tiny seeds inside scraped into the mixture, to infuse flavour into custard and cream-based recipes. They offer a rich and rounded vanilla flavour.

vanilla bean paste

This store-bought paste is a convenient way to replace whole vanilla pods and is great in desserts. One teaspoon of paste substitutes for one vanilla pod.

vanilla extract

For a pure vanilla taste, use a good-quality extract, not an essence or imitation flavour, or a fresh vanilla pod or bean paste.

vinegar

balsamic
Originally from Modena in Italy, there are many varieties on the market ranging in quality and flavour. Aged balsamics are generally preferable. Also available in a milder white version, which is used in dishes where the colour is important.

balsamic glaze
A thick and syrupy reduction of balsamic vinegar and sugar available from supermarkets.

cider
Usually made from cider or apple must, cider vinegar has a golden amber hue and a sour appley flavour. Use it in dressings, marinades and chutneys.

rice wine
Made from fermenting rice or rice wine, rice vinegar is milder and sweeter than vinegars made by oxidising distilled alcohol or wine made from grapes. Rice wine vinegar is available in white (colourless to pale yellow), black and red varieties from Asian food stores and some supermarkets.

white balsamic
Traditional balsamic vinegar is made with red wine while this variety is made with white wine. It is milder in flavour and is not as sweet as its dark cousin. It is used in sauces and dressings when you don't want a dark balsamic to colour your dish.

white (cannellini) beans

These small, kidney-shaped beans are available from supermarkets either canned or in dried form. Dried beans need to be soaked overnight in water before cooking.

MARKED INGREDIENTS

aïoli
A garlic-flavoured mayonnaise that's a popular condiment in Spanish and French cuisines. You can find it in most delicatessens, or make it yourself.

ancho chillies
Dried ancho chillies are a sweet and smoky Mexican poblano pepper available from some supermarkets and online. They have a smouldering, smoky flavour that's great in slow-cooked dishes.

apple cider
When we refer to apple cider in our recipes, we mean dry alcoholic cider distilled from apples.

asian chilli jam
Thai condiment made from ginger, chilli, garlic and shrimp paste used in soups and stir-fries. It goes well with roasted meats, egg dishes and cheese and is often served in a dollop as a garnish. You can substitute with a Thai chilli paste.

bok choy
A mildly flavoured green vegetable also known as pak choi or Chinese white cabbage. Baby bok choy can be cooked whole, while it's best to separate the leaves and trim the white stalks from the larger variety.

caramelised onion relish
Sliced onion cooked slowly to release all its sugars and made even more intense in flavour by the addition of brown sugar and balsamic vinegar. It is sold in most supermarkets as a condiment.

cheese

burrata
An Italian stretched-curd cheese, similar to mozzarella, burrata has a creamy, milky centre. It's best served simply with a tomato and basil salad. It's available from delicatessens and some supermarkets.

goat's cheese & curd

Goat's milk has a tart flavour, so cheese made from it, sometimes labelled *chèvre*, has a sharp, slightly acidic taste. Immature goat's cheese is milder and creamier than mature cheese and is sometimes found labelled 'goat's curd', which is smooth and spreadable. Goat's cheese is also available in more mature hard and soft varieties.

Gruyére

Firm cow's milk cheese with a smooth ivory interior and a natural brushed rind. Popular in Switzerland as a table cheese and cooked into fondues, gratins and quiches. It makes a fabulous melting cheese, especially in a sandwich.

labne

Middle Eastern cheese made from strained yoghurt from cow's milk. It's soft, creamy and spreadable, often in balls and marinated in chilli, herbs and oil.

ricotta salata

Made by pressing, salting, drying and aging fresh ricotta, is firm and salty and can be grated and shaved. You can substitute with feta or pecorino.

smoked mozzarella

Made by taking fresh mozzarella and cold smoking it over wood chips, this cheese takes on a distinctive brown colour and smoky flavour.

stracchino

A rindless, tender Italian cow's milk cheese that's eaten young and fresh and is great for melting. You can substitute with mozzarella or soft rind cheese.

chinese roasted duck

Available from any Chinatown, a ready-roasted duck is a perfect cheat for pies, salads, pancakes and more. The ducks are roasted and glazed in a combination of soy sauce, sugar and spices to give them their distinctive colour and flavour.

chinese cooking wine (shaoxing)

Similar to dry sherry, Shaoxing or Chinese cooking wine is a blend of glutinous rice, millet, a special yeast and the local spring waters of Shaoxing, where it is made, in northern China. It is sold in the Asian section of your supermarket and in Asian grocery stores.

chinese five-spice powder

A blend of cinnamon, Sichuan pepper, star anise, clove and fennel seeds, five spice is a popular seasoning for duck and pork. Available at Asian food stores and supermarkets.

chipotle chilli

This is a dried, smoked version of a jalapeño pepper, with a distinct medium–hot flavour and a lovely smoky note. They must be soaked in water before using.

chorizo

Firm, spicy, coarse-textured Spanish pork sausage seasoned with pepper, paprika and chillies. Available fresh and dried from supermarkets.

coconut

cream

The cream that rises to the top after the first pressing of coconut milk. Coconut cream is a rich, sweet liquid that is both higher in energy and fat than regular coconut milk. A common ingredient in curries and Asian sweets.

desiccated

Desiccated coconut is coconut meat which has been shredded and dried to remove the moisture. It's unsweeteend and very powdery. Great for baking as well as savoury Asian sauces and sambals.

flaked

Coconut flakes have a large shape and chewier texture than the desiccated variety and are often used for decorating and in cereals and baking.

milk

A milky, sweet liquid made by soaking grated fresh coconut flesh or desiccated coconut in warm water and squeezing through muslin or cheesecloth to extract the liquid. Available in tins or freeze-dried from supermarkets, coconut milk should not be confused with coconut juice, which is a clear liquid found inside young coconuts.

cream

The fat content determines the names of the different types of cream and their uses.

single

Has a butter fat content of at least 18 per cent. It is the type of cream most commonly used for making ice-cream, panna cotta and custard.

double

Often called heavy cream, this has a butter fat content of at least 48 per cent. It is usually served on the side of warm puddings or rich cakes. It can also be whipped to a thick consistency. Often called pouring cream.

whipping

This cream must contain at least 35 per cent fat. It doesn't whip as thickly as double cream.

curd

Lemon or passionfruit curds are made by thickening whole eggs, butter and the fruit juice to produce a sweet spread. Great for slices, tarts and pies. You can make your own or buy it in jars.

dashi

Classic and clear Japanese soup stock used as a base for miso and other broths. It's commonly made by boiling kelp (seaweed) and shaved bonito (fish). You can buy dashi in powder form from Asian supermarkets.

dukkah

A Middle Eastern nut and spice blend available from some supermarkets. Great for sprinkling on meats and salads or using in a spice crust.

dulce de leche

This is a thick South American milk caramel made by slowly heating and thickening sweetened milk. You can buy it in jars and use it to fill biscuits, pies, tarts and more. You can also make your own cheat's version by baking sweetened condensed milk.

fish sauce

An amber-coloured liquid drained from salted, fermented fish and used to add flavour to Thai and Vietnamese dishes such as curries and in dressings for salads. There are different grades available.

gochujang

A traditional Korean soy bean and chilli paste used as a condiment with soups and meats. You can find it at Asian supermarkets and grocery stores.

harissa

A North African condiment, harissa is a hot red paste made from chilli, garlic and spices including coriander, caraway and cumin. It may also contain tomato. Available in jars and tubes from supermarkets and specialty food stores, harissa enlivens tagines and couscous dishes and can be added to dressings, sauces and marinades.

juniper berries

The aromatic and bitter dried berries of a hardy evergreen bush, juniper is used for pickling vegetables and flavouring sauces. It goes well with duck and pork.

kaffir lime leaves

Fragrant leaves with a distinctive double-leaf structure, used crushed or shredded in Thai dishes. Available fresh or dried from Asian food stores and supermarkets.

laksa paste

A popular spicy Malaysian noodle soup, laksa is commonly made with a curry base. You can buy ready-made laksa paste from supermarkets and Asian grocery stores.

micro herbs

The baby version of edible herbs, these tiny edible leaves have a great intensity of flavour despite their size. Find them at farmers' markets and greengrocers.

mirin

A pale yellow Japanese cooking wine made from glutinous rice and alcohol. Sweet mirin is flavoured with corn syrup.

miso paste

A traditional Japanese ingredient produced by fermenting rice, barley or soy beans to a paste. It is used for sauces and spreads, pickling vegetables, and mixing with dashi stock to serve as miso soup. Red miso paste is robust while white miso paste is more delicate in flavour. Available from supermarkets and Asian food stores.

noodles
green tea

Made with buckwheat flour and green tea leaves, these distinctive green noodles have a pleasant texture and flavour. Find them sold dried at a Japanese grocer or substitute with plain soba noodles or rice noodles.

palm sugar

Produced by tapping the sap of palm trees, palm sugar is allowed to crystallise and is sold in cubes or round blocks, which you can shave and add to curries, dressings and Asian desserts. Available from supermarkets and Asian food stores.

pancetta

A cured Italian meat that is like prosciutto but less salty and with a softer texture. It's sold as thinly sliced pancetta strips or cubes of pancetta.

panko breadcrumbs

Made from crustless white bread, these breadcrumbs are extra flaky and crispy when fried. Great for schnitzel. Find them at Asian grocery stores and some supermarkets.

pastry
filo

Extremely thin sheets of pastry popular in Greek, Turkish and Middle Eastern baking, particularly for sweets such as baklava. It dries out quickly, so when working with it, keep sheets covered with a clean, damp tea towel.

shortcrust

A savoury or sweet pastry that is available ready-made in blocks and frozen sheets. If you can't find store-bought sweet shortcrust, simply sprinkle plain shortcrust liberally with sugar, or make your own.

225g plain flour
125g unsalted butter, chilled and cubed
3 egg yolks
1 tablespoon iced water

Place the flour and butter in the bowl of a food processor and process in short bursts until mixture resembles fine breadcrumbs. While the motor is running, add the egg yolks and water. Process until the dough just comes together. Turn dough out onto a lightly floured surface and gently bring together to form a ball. Using your hands, flatten dough into a disc. Cover in clingfilm and refrigerate. When ready to use, roll out on a lightly floured surface to 3mm thick. To make sweet shortcrust pastry, add 80g icing sugar.

peppercorns
green

Picked before they are fully ripe, green peppercorns are sold fresh or brined in tins. They are commonly used in a peppercorn gravy or sauce for steak.

Sichuan
Not a pepper, but dried berries with a spicy, tongue-tingling effect sold whole. Toast in a hot, dry frying pan until fragrant before crushing or grinding. It's a popular coating for salt and pepper squid.

pickled ginger
Also known as gari, this Japanese condiment is made from young ginger that's been pickled in sugar and vinegar. It's commonly served with sushi.

pomegranate molasses
A concentrated syrup with a sweet, tart flavour that's available from Middle Eastern grocery stores and specialty food stores. Great for salad dressings, meat rubs and sauces.

preserved lemon
Preserved lemons are lemons rubbed with salt, packed in jars, covered with lemon juice and left for about four weeks. They're often flavoured with cloves, cinnamon or chilli. Discard the flesh, rinse and chop the rind for use in cooking. They are popular in Moroccan cuisine, where they are added to tagines, and they also make a zesty salad dressing. Available from delicatessens and some supermarkets.

quince paste
Also known as *membrillo* for its Spanish origins, this intensely aromatic paste is made by boiling quinces, lemon juice and sugar to a thick condiment that teams well with cheeses and roasted meats such as duck and pork.

quinoa
Although quinoa looks like a grain, it's actually a seed originating from South America. Packed with protein, it has a chewy texture and nutty flavour and is fluffy when cooked. The most common variety is white, which is mild in taste, while the red variety has a stronger flavour and crunch. You can use it as you would couscous or rice.

ras el hanout
A spice mix literally translating to 'top of the shop', ras el hanout can contain over 20 different spices, most commonly cinnamon, cardamom, cloves, coriander, chilli, paprika and tumeric. Find it at most supermarkets. It makes a great rub for lamb.

semolina
A flour made from ground durum wheat, semolina is the base ingredient for pasta, breakfast cereal, porridge, sweet puddings and Middle Eastern cakes.

shichimi togarashi
A common Japanese spice mixture made from ground chilli, orange peel, sesame seeds and more. It is often sprinkled on soups and noodles. Find it at Asian supermarkets and grocery stores.

smoked paprika
Unlike Hungarian paprika, the Spanish style known as pimentón is deep and smoky in flavour. It is made from smoked, ground pimento peppers and comes in varying intensities from sweet and mild (dulce), bittersweet medium hot (agridulce) and hot (picante).

speck
Speck is a slab of German-style smoked and cured ham and is available from delicatessens. If unavailable, you can use bacon or sliced pancetta instead.

sumac
Dried berries of a flowering plant are ground to produce an acidic reddish-purple powder popular in the Middle East. Sumac has a slight lemony flavour and is great sprinkled in salads or on dips.

tahini paste
A thick paste made from ground sesame seeds. Used in Middle Eastern cooking, it is available in jars and tins from supermarkets and health food shops. It is used to make the popular dip hummus.

thai curry paste
Buy good-quality pastes in jars from Asian food stores or the supermarket. When trying a new brand, it is a good idea to add a little at a time to test the heat as the chilli intensity can vary significantly from brand to brand.

tofu
Literally translated as 'bean curd', tofu is made by coagulating the milk of soy beans and pressing the curd into blocks. Tofu comes in several grades according to the amount of moisture that has been removed. Silken tofu is the softest, with a custard-like texture. Soft tofu is slightly firmer, while dried or firm tofu has the texture of, and cuts like, a semi-hard cheese such as haloumi. Usually sold in the refrigerated section of supermarkets.

tzatziki
A Greek dip made from thick, plain yoghurt, garlic and chopped or grated cucumber, sometimes with dill or mint added. Available in supermarkets, it can be used as a sauce for grilled meat and seafood or served as an accompaniment to savoury pastries.

wasabi
A very hot Japanese paste similar to horseradish, wasabi is used in making sushi and as a condiment. It's available from Asian food stores and supermarkets.

wonton wrappers
Chinese in origin, these square or round thin sheets of dough are available fresh or frozen from Asian stores. They can be steamed or fried. Fill with meat and vegetables to make dumplings for soup or use as a base for nibbles, or deep-fry or bake, sprinkled with sugar for dessert.

za'atar
Middle Eastern spice mix containing dried herbs, sesame seeds and sumac. Often used as a crust for grilled and baked meats.

GLOBAL MEASURES

*Measures vary from Europe
to the US and even from
Australia to NZ.*

metric and imperial

Measuring cups and spoons may vary
slightly from one country to another,
but the difference is generally not
sufficient to affect a recipe.

One metric teaspoon holds 5ml. In North
America and the UK we use 15ml
(3-teaspoon) tablespoons, however, in
Australia 1 tablespoon holds 20ml
(4 teaspoons).

LIQUIDS AND SOLIDS

*Measuring cups and spoons
and a set of scales are great
assets in the kitchen.*

liquids

cup	metric	imperial
⅛ cup	30ml	1 fl oz
¼ cup	60ml	2 fl oz
⅓ cup	80ml	2½ fl oz
½ cup	125ml	4 fl oz
⅔ cup	160ml	5 fl oz
¾ cup	180ml	6 fl oz
1 cup	250ml	8 fl oz
2 cups	500ml	16 fl oz
2¼ cups	560ml	20 fl oz
4 cups	1 litre	32 fl oz

solids

metric	imperial
20g	½ oz
60g	2 oz
125g	4 oz
180g	6 oz
250g	8 oz
500g	16 oz (1 lb)
1kg	32 oz (2 lb)

MADE TO MEASURE

*Equivalents for metric
and imperial measures
and ingredient names.*

millimetres to inches

metric	imperial
3mm	⅛ inch
6mm	¼ inch
1cm	½ inch
2.5cm	1 inch
5cm	2 inches
18cm	7 inches
20cm	8 inches
23cm	9 inches
25cm	10 inches
30cm	12 inches

ingredient equivalents UK/US

aubergine	eggplant
bicarbonate soda	baking soda
caster sugar	superfine sugar
celeriac	celery root
chickpeas	garbanzos
coriander	cilantro
cornflour	cornstarch
cos lettuce	romaine lettuce
courgette	zucchini
mange tout	snow pea
pepper	bell pepper
plain flour	all-purpose flour
rocket	arugula
self-raising flour	self-rising flour
spring onion	scallion

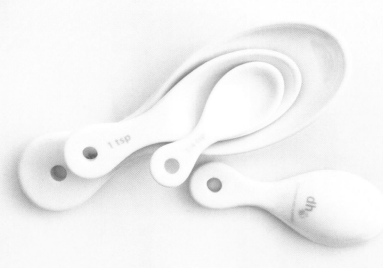

OVEN TEMPERATURE

Setting the oven to the right temperature can be critical when making baked goods.

celsius to fahrenheit

celsius	fahrenheit
100°C	200°F
120°C	250°F
140°C	275°F
150°C	300°F
160°C	325°F
180°C	350°F
190°C	375°F
200°C	400°F
220°C	425°F

electric to gas

celsius	gas
110°C	¼
130°C	½
140°C	1
150°C	2
170°C	3
180°C	4
190°C	5
200°C	6
220°C	7
230°C	8
240°C	9
250°C	10

BUTTER AND EGGS

Let 'fresh is best' be your mantra when it comes to selecting dairy goods.

butter

For baking we generally use unsalted butter as it lends a sweeter flavour. Either way, the impact is minimal. Salted butter has a longer shelf life and is preferred by some people.

eggs

Unless otherwise indicated we use large (60g) chicken eggs. To preserve freshness, store eggs in the refrigerator in the carton they are sold in. Use only the freshest eggs in recipes such as mayonnaise or dressings that use raw or barely cooked eggs. Be extra cautious if there is a salmonella problem in your community, particularly in food that is to be served to children, the elderly or pregnant women.

THE BASICS

Here are some simple weight conversions for cups of common ingredients.

common ingredients

ground almonds
1 cup | 120g
brown sugar
1 cup | 175g
white sugar
1 cup | 220g
caster sugar
1 cup | 220g
icing sugar
1 cup | 160g
plain or self-raising flour
1 cup | 150g
fresh breadcrumbs
1 cup | 70g
finely grated Parmesan cheese
1 cup | 80g
uncooked rice
1 cup | 200g
cooked rice
1 cup | 165g
uncooked couscous
1 cup | 200g
cooked, shredded chicken, pork or beef
1 cup | 160g
olives
1 cup | 150g

THANK YOU

A book is such a huge production and I am extremely lucky to have a very talented team around me to help bring it to life. To photographer Will Meppem, thank you for your beautiful eye and your calm and patient nature – you are a true wizard of your craft.

For all things creative, I can't thank my über-talented art director, Chi Lam, enough; everything you touch is magic. To the German mistress of words, Melanie Hansche, I am always happy to be in your efficient and capable company. Thank you for your perfectly written prose and editing.

For all things food – testing, chopping, baking, frying, roasting and preparing – Hannah Meppem, you are definitely one in a million. Thank you for sharing my values in perfection and for making every recipe, every chop and dice, and every bite amazing. To Alice Storey, who helped test many of the recipes, thank you for your tenacity in making sure they worked perfectly.

Many thanks also for the support and wisdom of my long-time publisher, Shona Martyn, and her amazing sidekick, Catherine Milne, at HarperCollins, who have unwavering faith in me.

To the unsung hero, Tony Houssarini, who works in prepress production making sure every image in the book is perfect – thank you for your hard work and amazing eye. My inspiring magazine team, you are my rock who keep all the wheels moving while I'm absorbed in the book world – thank you for all your patience.

It goes without saying I thank my family and friends (you know who you are and you also know how much I love you and appreciate your support), and lastly to the absolute loves of my life, my little boys, Angus and Tom, thank you for making life fun, interesting, challenging and grounding.

Thank you to the following suppliers for the loan of their wares:
Bassike, KitchenAid, Le Creuset, Paige Denim, Smeg.

BIO

At the age of eight, Donna Hay skipped into a kitchen, picked up a mixing bowl and never looked back. She later moved to the world of magazine test kitchens and publishing, where she established her trademark style of simple, smart and seasonal recipes all beautifully put together and photographed. It is food for every cook, every food lover, every day and every occasion.

Her unique style turned her into an international food-publishing phenomenon as a bestselling author of 23 cookbooks, publisher of the bi-monthly *donna hay magazine* and the number one iPad app in Australia, newspaper columnist, creator of the donna hay for Royal Doulton homewares collection plus a food range, and owner of her online store. Donna is a working mum to two beautiful boys.

Donna's first television series, Donna Hay – *fast, fresh, simple.*, a 13-part half-hour cooking series for Foxtel's The LifeStyle Channel in Australia and various international networks, brought her approach to food to life for viewers in over 14 countries.

Books by Donna Hay include: *the new classics*; *Fresh and Light*; *simple dinners*; *a cook's guide*; *fast, fresh simple.*; *Seasons*; *no time to cook*; *off the shelf*; *instant entertaining*; and the *simple essentials* collection.

donnahay.com.au

donnahay.com.au

Jump online and discover a world of Donna Hay, from more cookbooks and inspiring recipes for weeknights and weekends, to the latest magazine news and a shop of beautiful homewares, including her collection for Royal Doulton.

Plus, connect with Donna on Facebook, Instagram and Twitter.